"Dr. Self has the mind of a scholar, the heart of a pastor, and the voice of a prophet. *Flourishing Churches and Communities* is a holistic vision of the kind of seven-days-a-week discipleship our churches, communities, and corporations are dying to experience. This is an excellent blueprint for how the Holy Spirit is preparing to revitalize our people, relationships, and systems. Don't miss out on what God is about to do!"

Ernest N. Prabhakar, community evangelist
Kingsway Ministries, San Jose, CA

"Dr. Charles Self has created a well-conceived primer for anyone interested in helping a local congregation and the community in which it resides flourish in its health and prosperity. This book provides a well-rounded and theologically grounded understanding of how faith *and* work conspire to transform lives and communities."

Randy C. Walls, director of continuing education
Assemblies of God Theological Seminary

"Finally, a thoroughly Pentecostal consideration of how the heart, head, and hands can be mobilized by the Holy Spirit to empower vocational witness to the gospel to the ends of the earth. Inspiring testimonials— "profiles in courage"—work in tandem with the brilliant synoptic overview of the salvation history message from Genesis through Revelation to show how our faith, work, and economic lives can be of Spirit-inspired service to and anticipate the coming reign of God! Charlie Self shows the way forward for Pentecostal mission, evangelism, and discipleship in the twenty-first century."

Amos Yong, professor of theology
Regent University School of Divinity

"Charlie Self is an encourager of the church who contributes distinctive insights with a distinguished character. His voice is a thoughtful addition to the dialogue for building authentic Christian community."

Cherith Fee Nordling, associate professor of theology
Northern Seminary

"The integration of faith, life, and vocation as Christ-followers is the whole-life discipleship challenge of the twenty-first century. Dr. Charlie Self personally embodies the essence of that call. He is both scholar and pastor, theologian and practitioner, thinker and activist. His vision of the role of the Spirit and the church working together to grow disciples past the unbiblical dichotomy between the spiritual and the secular is compelling and needed. I highly recommend this work to you."

James Bradford, secretary-treasurer
General Council of the Assemblies of God (USA)

"Secular humanists seem determined to confine Christianity to a church building—inside four walls. They are uncomfortable when Christianity spills into the marketplace and becomes a cultural architect, affecting the design and activity of social, educational, and political institutions. Dr. Self affirms the necessity of integrating the 'lifestyle of Christ' into every aspect of life. There is no dichotomy between evangelism and discipleship, ministry and work, economic transformation and faith, grace and justice. This book is a must-read. If the principles taught in it are practiced, the body of Christ will become the force God created it to be."

Alton Garrison, assistant general superintendent
General Council of the Assemblies of God (USA)

"Pentecostals are proven entrepreneurs. Their dedicated, creative efforts to share timeless biblical truth have resulted in one of the broadest expansions of Christianity in history. Charlie Self, in *Flourishing Churches and Communities*, helps Pentecostals to carefully reflect about the biblical foundation of the worldview they have been living out for over a century."

Darrin J. Rodgers, director
Flower Pentecostal Heritage Center

"I have known Charlie Self for twenty years. The truths he shares in this primer reflect a long and honest journey of making faith relevant and vibrant in all arenas of life. This book begins to remove bricks from the unacceptable walls we have not only erected but institutionalized between work and worship, business and ministry, clergy and laity, pulpit and marketplace."

Brett Johnson, president
The Institute for Innovation, Integration & Impact

"I am overwhelmed by the eternal canvas Charlie Self has painted in his new book, *Flourishing Churches and Communities*. You unpack and then paint in layers a beautiful piece of art as the Old Testament and the New Testament unfold. I stand back and finally see clearly how the Lord, through his Word, has led me to worship him and to serve him in my work. Every church needs to use this book in equipping their leaders and their congregations. The wisdom in this book can help God's people look for the frequency of faith that will affect their world of work and see miracles happen, especially at this time when so many people are looking for jobs."

Jack Reeves, educational administrator and lay leader

"This engagingly written and irenic work encourages us to integrate the entire sphere of life under Jesus' lordship and for God's glory. Some of us struggle with backgrounds in which only a narrow range of activities count as 'spiritual' and the rest of life appears devoid of God's presence, but Self shows how a wide range of life, work, and thought should honor God, as in Colossians 3:23."

Craig Keener, professor of New Testament
Asbury Theological Seminary

"There are very few men who combine the highest level of biblical teaching and study with powerful Holy Spirit ministry, humble servanthood, and overflowing love for people and community. Along with congregations across the country, Dr. Self is a trusted kingdom teacher and model to our congregation of the Spirit-filled life and mission. In his ministry and in this book, Dr. Self brings clarity and deeper understanding to the simplicity, practicality, and beauty of what the church can truly be to the world around it."

Shawn Franco, lead pastor
Cornerstone Assembly of God, Richmond, VA

"My colleague Charlie Self has demonstrated his giftings again in this book. Integrating theology with the daily life realities of economics for the purpose of discipleship is close to the heart of his calling. My specialty is the Old Testament and I found his overview of the Old Testament foundation for this integration to be excellent. Charlie gets right to the key principles and concepts, and I agree with his understanding of these. He has a wonderful grasp of the big picture and articulately presents it. At times I wished I had written what he wrote. This book makes a significant biblical-theological contribution to the discussion."

Roger Cotton, professor of Old Testament
Assemblies of God Theological Seminary

FLOURISHING CHURCHES & COMMUNITIES

Primers in This Series

Economic Shalom: *A Reformed Primer on Faith, Work, and Human Flourishing*

Flourishing Churches and Communities: *A Pentecostal Primer on Faith, Work, and Economics for Spirit-Empowered Discipleship*

Flourishing Faith: *A Baptist Primer on Work, Economics, and Civic Stewardship*

How God Makes the World a Better Place: *A Wesleyan Primer on Faith, Work, and Economic Transformation*

FLOURISHING CHURCHES & COMMUNITIES

A Pentecostal Primer on Faith, Work, and Economics for Spirit-Empowered Discipleship

CHARLIE SELF

With a Foreword by George O. Wood

GRAND RAPIDS · MICHIGAN

ISBN 978-1-938948-16-9

Christian's Library Press
An imprint of the Acton Institute for the Study of Religion & Liberty
98 E. Fulton
Grand Rapids, Michigan 49503
www.clpress.com

Cover design by DO MORE GOOD
Interior design by Sharon VanLoozenoord
Editing by Stephen J. Grabill, Timothy J. Beals, and Andrew Sloan

21 20 19 18 17 16 15   2 3 4 5 6 7 8 9 10

Printed in the United States of America
First edition

Contents

Foreword

In just one century, Pentecostal Christianity has grown from a series of scattered revivals to a movement of hundreds of millions of passionate biblical believers dedicated to Spirit-empowered fulfillment of the Great Commission. In addition to fostering hundreds of fellowships and networks, Pentecostal vitality and mission have permeated every tradition of global Christianity. It is exciting to see that Pentecostals have moved from the margins to the epicenter of Christianity. From the first prayer meetings in the 1890s to the Azusa Street Revival, from the Bible Women of India to the revivals in Chile, this fresh force for evangelization continues to make its mark for the glory of God.

My fellowship, the Assemblies of God (USA), is about to enter its centennial year. What began in 1914 with a few leaders in Hot Springs, Arkansas, has grown to a global movement of over sixty-five million adherents in more than two hundred nations today. We are excited about our future and the future of our sister movements that are passionate about completing the Great Commission. We are also delighted to be part of the broader work of missionary Christianity. The Assemblies of God (USA) was one of the founding fellowships of the National Association of Evangelicals (NAE) in 1943. Pentecostals are active in the Lausanne Movement, excited about seeing the whole church take the whole gospel to the whole world.

For the past century, Pentecostals have emphasized equipping all of God's people for ministry, and there are hundreds of schools and training centers around the world where pastors, evangelists, and missionaries are preparing for their part in the harvest. As part of our growth and maturity, we have developed colleges and universities that contribute to the global conversations in a variety of biblical, historical, missiological, and theological disciplines. One of our notable contributions to the body of Christ is "knowledge on fire"—we aim to educate and empower scholar-practitioners who exemplify intellectual excellence united with a love for the church and a passion for mission.

This new work by Dr. Charlie Self is an important contribution to the church, as he presents an integration of faith, work, and economics in the context of the Great Commission mandate to make disciples. I am pleased to see his insightful and practical use of the Bible, church history, and contemporary stories of Christians to help our local churches become centers of transformation in their neighborhoods, our nation, and around the world. Charlie is putting into print what our most creative and innovative leaders have done for over a century—listening to the Holy Spirit and bringing the gospel to people through proclamation and demonstration of love and truth.

The Assemblies of God and most biblical Christians are deeply committed to evangelism, worship, discipleship, and compassion. We believe in the empowering work of the Spirit enabling the whole church to bring the whole gospel to the whole world. What Charlie does is remind pastors and spiritual leaders that this extraordinary work of Christ takes place through "ordinary" people who spend most of their waking hours working. Even more, by taking on economics Dr. Self is compelling us to see our participation in the local, national, and global economy as a positive part of God's plan to provide for the world. Charlie rightly affirms the paramount priorities of gospel proclamation and the sacred call to ministry. He is not dethroning spiritual leaders, but elevating all of God's people to their rightful place as royal priests, called to worship and witness (1 Peter 2:9–10).

I am especially pleased that the local church is the focus

of this work. Whether large or small, rural or urban, wealthy or working class, it is God's design to use the local church as his main agency for making disciples and transforming the community. The principles and stories in this book will be helpful to all pastors, staff, church boards, and leadership teams.

When I became superintendent, I articulated five core values to guide our fellowship into the future. Variations of these are shared by Christian leaders around the world. *Flourishing Churches and Communities* affirms and integrates all of the values. The first value is passionate proclamation of the gospel in word and deed. Dr. Self makes sure the reader knows that the Great Commission is at the forefront of the church's mission. Strategic investment in the next generation is the second. This includes educating future leaders in an integrated vision of discipleship and seeing God raise up Spirit-filled disciples in all domains. Third, we are committed to vigorously planting new churches and revitalizing existing ones. The insights in this primer will help church planters establish their mission and vision and assist our struggling congregations with fresh insights for their future. Imagine the impact of a local church whose members start new businesses, serve as educational and social leaders, and volunteer in other agencies of compassion—even as they build strong church ministries. Our fourth value, skillful resourcing of our fellowship, will only happen if God's people are listening to the Holy Spirit, creating value for others, and generating wealth that can be stewarded wisely.

Finally, none of these values can be realized apart from our fellowship's fifth core value—that God's people are fervently praying for his favor and help. Dr. Self's passion for prayer and spiritual awakening is compelling. I am especially moved by this passage:

> God uses individuals to spark revival and reformation in every era. Today we may be witnessing something new. Rather than pointing to one individual or movement as the "bonfire" of presence and power, perhaps the Holy Spirit is lighting

thousands—even millions—of "brush fires" as thoughtful Christians find each other, seek the face of God, and respond to the Spirit's call to holy, integrated living that transforms individuals and societies. The synergy of Trinitarian theology, repentant reflection on the state of Christian living, and mutual listening to Scripture, history, and the current wind of the Spirit has the potential to awaken the church and stabilize society. The question for Pentecostals is simple: Are we ready to assume a place of economic and social responsibility without sacrificing the urgency of evangelization?

Our sovereign God uses fervent prayer to light these brush fires.

I commend this book to all Christians who desire spiritual and social renewal in the power of the Spirit. I urge Pentecostal clergy and lay leaders to prayerfully study these insights and discover how the Holy Spirit is leading their local church. Finally, I am delighted that Charlie is part of our fellowship and building bridges of cooperation and friendship with other Christian communions. Pentecostalism as a historical stream may only be a century old, but our heritage and the wellsprings that feed the river of our vitality are part of the church Jesus has been building for nearly two thousand years.

George O. Wood, general superintendent
General Council of the Assemblies of God (USA)
Chairman, World Assemblies of God Fellowship
Advisory committee, Pentecostal World Fellowship

Preface

Scotty's Story

Scotty is every pastor's dream of an ideal church member. A mechanic by trade, Scotty owns an independent shop in Campbell, California—in the heart of Silicon Valley. He and his family are active in Bethel Church of San Jose, serving on committees and production teams, teaching, helping out with special-needs children, and enjoying fellowship with others. He is active in Christian bass-fishing tournaments, through which he has seen many come to Christ. He is cheerful, hardworking, and has a great reputation in the community. Scotty seeks to honor the Lord in all he does.

By most measures of Christian discipleship, Scotty is exactly what all churches need. He loves God, reads the Bible, and attends church faithfully, gives his money and time generously, and enjoys the respect of his colleagues and neighbors. Scotty is indeed an exemplary disciple—but there is more to this story!

What is missing from the discipleship accounts of most believers is the fact that Scotty's full-time "ministry" and greatest kingdom service takes place during the sixty-plus hours a week he and his wife, Patti, devote to their business. Scotty's Automotive is not merely a secular means to a sacred end. The business is the mission, contributing directly to the flourishing of the community and economy in ways the church rarely measures. Consider these concrete realities:

❖ Scotty's Automotive helps feed, clothe, and house forty-plus people because he employs six other mechanics. Each of these families participates in the community and economy: working, spending, and giving of their time to serve others.

❖ Hundreds of people bring their cars to Scotty's shop each month. They come in crisis, needing help in order to tend to their daily affairs. His successful repairs enable folks to offer thousands of productive hours of work that would be lost if their cars remained unrepaired or required frequent returns. Beyond just work, Scotty enables families to take vacations safely, get to church and sporting events, and carry out charitable and cultural activities because their cars are sound.

❖ Scotty says that he and his team possess about the same volume of knowledge as a general physician. With computers, changing technology, and ongoing training, the day of the "shade-tree mechanic" has essentially passed.

❖ Let's go further. Scotty pays his taxes, thus contributing (with some grumbling about how the money is spent) to the social good. He pays into workers' compensation and health care benefits, directly and indirectly supporting the medical community. The rent he pays for his large building space provides income for the landlord that eventually finds its way back into the economy.

The ripple effect of one family business represents much more than a job that allows a couple to tithe and pay their bills. Scotty and his team are connected with millions of dollars in the local economy, and their efforts contribute to a flourishing community. In the midst of all this, they have led many to Christ, strengthened the faith of others, and offered a sterling witness to neighbors who aren't involved in the church. Scotty has quietly helped several struggling families with reduced-cost repairs. He makes sure his customers are safe, and he never does work unless it is needed.

Why is Scotty's story important? Because it touches on every major theme is this book. Making disciples is the content of the Great Commission. Godly character, healthy relationships, and vocational clarity are vital for every believer, every local church, and the larger body of Christ to fulfill their purpose. Spiritual leaders are dedicated to seeing church members grow as they reach out to their community and glorify Christ by allowing the Holy Spirit to use them.

The missing piece in our discipleship is the integration of faith, work, and economics so that Christians are not only ethical and excellent at work but see their work as part of God's larger design for their community, state, and nation to flourish! This work is designed to correct this gap and empower Spirit-filled leaders with tools to equip local churches as powerful places of the presence of God and as communities that commission members to see their work as worship and the flourishing of the community as part of the Great Commission. Each person's daily work is their ministry before God and a watching world.

As Pentecostal believers, we are urgent about the Great Commission (Matt. 28:18–20; Acts 1:8) and rely on the power of the Holy Spirit to go across the street and around the world. We expect supernatural signs to confirm the preaching of the gospel and we affirm that all believers—regardless of age, class, ethnicity, or gender—can be empowered by the Spirit to fulfill the mission of God as we prepare for the soon return of Christ.

As we go into the world, we are led by the Spirit to create charities, dig wells, offer medical help, develop educational institutions, care for the outcasts, and even start businesses to provide resources or open doors in "closed" situations. All these efforts need to continue and grow.

The focus of this book is to see work and economic transformation as intentional and integral to Christian discipleship and the mission of the local church.

As Martin Luther's great hymn, "*A Mighty Fortress Is Our God,*" declares in the last verse, "The Spirit and the gifts are ours." Pentecostals now number in the tens of millions in the United States and in the hundreds of millions around the world, encompassing all cultures and permeating all Christian traditions. Our movement, though now a century old, shows no signs of slowing; and for this we must thank God for his sovereign grace and merciful outpourings.

The passion and urgency of mission must be joined with the panorama of the purpose of God so that we completely fulfill the plan of God in our day. Spirit-filled Christianity touches all of life. Living in the power of the Holy Spirit includes active participation in the economy, work as worship, and "providential increases" (John Wesley) in the influence of the kingdom of God.

Scotty's story is repeated many times over by faithful followers of Christ. Our aim is to help believers become aware of and energized by the connection between their faith and work, and between their personal and social influence.

Scotty's story is part of a larger divine drama that is God's eternal purpose to glorify himself in the story of his relationship with humankind. God's story is majestic and mysterious, boundless yet occurring in real places and through real people. When our stories align with the Lord's, something beautiful happens: God's people become the source of his "manifold" (colorful, many-splendored) wisdom on display to the universe (Eph. 3:10).

Study Questions

1. When you hear the words *economics* and *economy*, what thoughts come to mind? How are these words connected with your present understanding of God's work in the world?

2. What impressed you the most about Scotty's story? What questions does it raise in your mind?

3. How do most people in your church view their daily work, whether in business, at home, at school, or as volunteers?

4. Bonus question: How do we measure spiritual growth?

For Further Reading

Forster, Greg. "Theology That Works," 2012. Available at the Oikonomia Network website, www.oikonomianetwork.org.

Hewitt, Les, and Charlie Self. *The Power of Faithful Focus.* Deerfield, FL: Faith Communications, 2004.

Johnson, Brett. *Convergence.* Saratoga, CA: Indaba Publishing, 2010.

Zimmermann, Jens. *Incarnational Humanism: A Philosophy of Culture for the Church in the World.* Downers Grove, IL: InterVarsity, 2012.

Introduction

The Courage to Flourish

"God begins with a Garden and ends with a City."   **Ray Bakke**

"The central purpose and ultimate aim of universal history is the kingdom of God established by Jesus Christ. This is not an afterthought of God or a subsequent emendation of the plan of creation. . . . It is the beginning, middle and end of all of God's ways and works."

Philip Schaff, 1890

"Today, millions of churchgoers are 'Christians' for only a few hours a week. Christianity is a leisure time activity for them rather than a complete way of life. The withering of discipleship is one of the gravest threats facing the church in our time.

"The main cause of the problem is that churches have disconnected discipleship from everyday life. . . .

"We urgently need to recover the calling to whole-life discipleship. The largest portion of life—our work in the home and in our jobs—is excluded from our concept of discipleship and stewardship. Most churches have nothing spiritually powerful to offer for the activities that define most of our daily lives during the other six days of the week."

Greg Forster, "Theology That Works"

If you are reading this book, you are most likely a person of influence—perhaps a pastor of a church, a member of the board, or a small group leader. You are a woman or a man committed to following Christ in every area of your life. You want your fellow church members to enjoy the same fulfillment that comes from loving obedience to the Word of God. You get excited when converts are baptized, people are filled with the Spirit, the gifts flow in your services, marriages are restored, addicts are healed, and young people receive a call to missions. You take time every day to read your Bible and pray for others.

If you are a Bible study leader or pastor, you are always preparing for your next message. Your bookshelves are filled with classical and contemporary Christian literature—some of which you have actually read. You try to eat with your family most nights, and your battle with your waistline is a draw at the moment. Finances are tight in the church and at home, but through your tithing, saving, and careful budgeting, it looks like your church and family will weather the current storm.

You pay attention to headlines and political trends, but you wonder how much good all the agitation does in light of the breakdown of private and public virtue and the real-life problems of the people you encounter. You know that the Lord cares about the economy and the legal system. You want good people in Hollywood and your local hospital. You pray that some of your church youth group members will go to a good university, keeping their faith and making a difference for Christ.

In the midst of all this, you watch the Middle East and ponder if it is all going to end with bombs flying from Iran to Israel, with Chinese and Russian armies hungry for oil and power converging on the region. Maybe you need to find a piece of land outside your city, build a bunker, buy a supply of dried food, and procure water purification equipment. As you contemplate all of this, your eyes are drawn to a beautiful painting in a local gallery and your spouse is enamored with the athleticism of the acrobats you just saw at the local sports arena. Then you consider why these "worldly" thoughts cross your mind at all, when billions of people need to hear the gospel and receive basic necessities. And your neighbor needs a job. In fact, the altars of the church are flooded with women and men requesting prayer as a result of unemployment and financial crises.

In the midst of these competing thoughts, you look at the

lives of most members of your community and wonder if there is more to the Christian life than personal piety and good Christian ethics at home and at work. You have attended a couple of breakfasts with business leaders who speak about "Marketplace Ministry" as the cutting edge of evangelism and missions. These are exciting thoughts, but the business leaders' barely concealed contempt for clergy and the relevance of the local church causes some red flags to wave in your mind.

Every month you attend a prayer meeting with the local pastors. The good news is that some wonderful prayer takes place and the leaders genuinely desire to work together to reach your region for Christ. You also notice the divide between the leaders of larger and smaller churches. The former attend less often, sending subordinates in their stead. In spite of all this, some initiatives for prayer and outreach are making progress and the evangelical and Pentecostal churches are talking to each other. Your church is "healthy," and some fellow lay and clerical leaders are making a difference. So why is there a gnawing disquiet inside? Why do you wake up in the middle of night with the thought that there must be more to this kingdom life reverberating in your heart?

Inside, there is a longing to remove the "disconnects" between Sunday and the rest of the week, between faith and work, between individual ethics and the economy of the community, state, and nation. You know this shouldn't be left to politicians and secular experts, but what is the church to do?

This book is for you and for all serious followers of Jesus Christ. It doesn't represent a secret formula that divulges hidden truths for the spiritual elite. This is a primer on discipleship that connects faith, work, and economics within a biblical, Trinitarian framework of Spirit-empowered living for the glory of God and the fulfillment of the Great Commission.

The triune God is sovereign over all dimensions of life. Service to Christ takes place in all domains, from parenthood to pastoral care, from business leadership to artistic endeavors. Stop reading now if you want to continue on your current well-worn pathways. But if you suspect that there is more to following Jesus and that God's people need to connect Sunday with the rest of their week, please keep reading.

What is measurable progress in Christian living? Put bluntly, spiritual leaders must define discipleship in a way that includes work and economic activity outside the church walls.

Before We Go Further

"The economy" in this book is not defined as a "school of economics" or focused on the policies of the Federal Reserve. These issues do matter, and Christian thinkers need to engage them. For the purpose of provoking biblical, Spirit-led change, here is a practical definition of the economy:

> The economy is the social system through which people organize their work and disperse its fruits. It includes employment and pay, property ownership, exchange, business, and investment. God created us as stewards of his world. God bestows daily opportunities for delighting in creation's beauty, discovering its wealth, and multiplying its blessings. A just economy with opportunity for all will respect the rule of law and be built on the foundations of personal liberty, moral virtue that is concerned for the community, and transcendent truth.

As we learn together, here are some things we are *not* doing in this book:

We are not trying to artificially fuse the Bible and Economics 101. We are not promoting an ideological or partisan agenda. We are not reducing life to economics. That is the Marxist-materialist error; a Christ-centered life is never just one-dimensional. But it is vital that we not privatize economic life, disconnecting one person's work from another. We must not spiritualize work as a mere means to an end—i.e., "I only work so I can tithe and give to the 'really important' work at the church." We are also not repudiating the special calling of ministers, as they equip believers and lead local churches.

Our aim is to elevate all believers to their proper place of "royal priesthood" (Ex. 19:6; 1 Peter 2:9–10), thereby creating flourishing churches and communities.

Now, one more thought before we continue . . . What is "work"?

Work in Scripture encompasses much more than salary or wage-earning activity. Therefore, work today includes what parents do at home, charitable activity, students being diligent at school, and a variety of other activities. Here is a synthesis of how the Bible views work:

> Work is all meaningful daily activity distinct from recreation and rest where we are fulfilling our purpose and contributing to the common good. For followers of Christ, work is all intentional activity that fulfills the Great Commandment and directly or indirectly contributes to the Great Commission. Our work is the daily offering of our whole lives as worship before God (Rom. 12:1–2).

Calling and Work

Understanding our callings before God and their contribution to the life of the world is very important. All people are called to repent, believe, and enjoy a relationship with the Trinity through the gospel of Jesus Christ. Calling also refers to the general call of all people to worship the Creator and be stewards of God's world (more about this below). All believers are also called to be witnesses of the good news, emissaries of grace to a world in need. So there are at least three ways to understand "calling."

Calling also refers to those God sets apart for leadership in the church and for the mission of the church. We will explore these specific callings more fully. At this juncture, however, we are affirming a distinction between a personal sense of vocation and the current occupation that fills our waking hours. Sometimes occupation (how we work) and vocation are the same, or at least very closely aligned in a person's life. Other times, they are more distinct. For example, a church-planting pastor may be an office manager while she pioneers the new work. Her "calling" is pastoral, while her days are filled with meaningful work, some of which may even be "pastoral" toward her workplace colleagues. God also calls people into one or more domains of influence. A man or a woman may be called to education, the arts, or media influence.

In this book we affirm the importance of all work through which God sends his people into the world as salt and light. What matters is that there are "no little people" (Francis Schaeffer) in God's plan and that one's current paycheck is not the sum of one's anointing!

An Unprecedented Moment

This primer stands in the flow of the current work of the Holy Spirit in the body of Christ. From calls for integration at the Lausanne Conference in Cape Town in 2010, to scores of new ministries promoting daily work as mission, there is a growing awareness among God's people that the Holy Spirit is initiating something new. The Acton Institute, cofounded by Father Robert Sirico and Kris Mauren, is devoted to the integration of Judeo-Christian truths with free-market principles of economics. Excellent Protestant thinkers have complemented Acton's Roman Catholic roots, thus enabling Acton to become an unprecedented incubator of relational ecumenism. Many of these Protestant influences hail from the Reformed tradition, representing centuries of reflection concerning the sovereignty of God over all spheres of life. Now we see several other evangelical traditions joining the conversation—and look out, world, here come the Pentecostals!

Here Come the Pentecostals!

Pentecostal Christianity is just over a century old as an identifiable movement, but the streams that feed this rushing river flow from every wellspring of Christian tradition. An honest look at American and global Christianity yields an awareness that much of the growing edge of God's work in the world is taking place through movements that are rooted in evangelical pietism, Wesleyan vision, and Pentecostal passion. *Pentecostals are not only evangelizing; they are building educational and social institutions that are contributing mature thinking to all the domains that concern thoughtful Christians.* As their churches grow, so does social mobility, the emergence of educational institutions, and increased social and political responsibilities.

The government of South Africa recently released the results of a ten-year study detailing the upward economic and social movement of women and men who were actively engaged in a local church. The effects of the gospel are profoundly positive. It is exciting to see devout, thoughtful Christians uniting to equip and empower the body of Christ for its work in the world—a work that is encapsulated in the Great Commandment (Matt. 22:37–40) and the Great Commission (Matt. 28:18–20).

The heart of Pentecostal identity is the present reality of the work of the Holy Spirit, who empowers all believers for gospel service. This includes the expectation of continual encounters with God that enrich calling and effectiveness and release believers to follow in the delivering, healing, and reconciling work of Jesus Christ.

Pentecostals are Bible-centered, passionate, and practical. They are the ultimate synthesizers of ideas and practices found in older traditions. Pentecostals affirm the empowering work of the Holy Spirit that enables believers, individually and in community, to live holy lives, with increasing evidence of virtue (see the fruit of the Spirit in Galatians 5:22–23 and the character traits of 2 Peter 1:3–8), joyous expression of the manifestations of the Spirit (1 Cor. 12–14), and evangelistic effectiveness. All this work takes place in the real world of commerce, raising families, politics, and all other expressions of human life. As we "connect the dots," we discover that *a biblical worldview empowered by the Spirit will foster discipleship that will create, refine, and sustain wise participation in the economy within an ethos of stewardship and the fulfillment of the Great Commission.*

Five Guiding Principles

Here are five guiding principles for the integration of faith, work, and economics that we will refer to again and again in the course of this book.

Principle One: Work is good.

Human beings are created in the image of God and bestowed with inherent dignity. God the Creator fashioned us for worship and work, to know God and to be stewards of his creation. Designed for relationships, men and women are not isolated beings—only finding their full sense of identity and purpose by uniting their efforts while participating in the economy so that all can prosper. Our Lord Jesus Christ forever dignified human life and purpose through his incarnation. Jesus of Nazareth, a real person in history, is the one and same risen Christ, who is the firstborn among many brothers and sisters. The same Holy Spirit who breathed life into Adam and Eve in the garden and anointed Jesus for his mission breathes new life into every regenerated Christian and bestows general and particular gifts upon communities and individuals to fulfill God's reconciling and redemptive purposes. All present activity is a convergence of creation and hope, integrating the creation order with the perfect order of the age to come.

Principle Two: Although sin has effaced human nature and work, it has not erased the divine nature in people and the ability to bring good to the world.

God's gifts of creativity and freewill are effaced but not eliminated, and therefore people have great freedom to bring good or ill to the world. Creative, self-aware activity is a universal blessing and a bridge between people of all faiths or none. God the Holy Spirit is active in the world, in both the common grace expressed in commerce, culture, and community and in the prevenient grace leading to salvation. Sin is personal and systemic and the cause of the inequities in economics and the injustices in government.

Principle Three: God has reconciled the world to himself in Christ and is now working through the church to express the life of the kingdom in the present age.

The Great Commission to make disciples of all nations includes Spirit-empowered economic activity that demonstrates the righteousness, peace, and joy of the kingdom. God the Redeemer liberates the church to live the future now, including helping communities and nations to flourish economically and socially. The death and resurrection of Christ enables believers to obey the Great

Commandment to love God with all our being and love our neighbor as ourselves. This is the summation of the ethical, relational, and vocational wholeness that is God's will for every Christian, church, and community. Discipleship unites the character, nature, and ways of God into a cohesive expression of transformation.

Principle Four: God the Holy Spirit actively energizes compassion for the poor and wealth creation for community flourishing.

Life is not intended to be a zero-sum game, with fear and scarcity driving decisions and limiting liberty. Wealth creation fuels generosity and is part of the human calling to be cocreators with God, stewards of the gifts and resources he has bestowed, and servants to all humankind. When God's empowering presence is recognized and the charisms of each believer are unleashed, the results are prosperity for all—those both inside and outside of the church. Wealth creation does not ignore creation-care or sound ecological stewardship. Caring for the earth is part of ensuring a prosperous future for upcoming generations. When Jesus said that the poor would always be present, he was not being fatalistic or laissez-faire about poverty and economic shalom. Jesus was being realistic, and his calls for sacrificial work for the poor remain the cure as God's people serve those who cannot return the favor.

Principle Five: Cultural, economic, and social institutions are built on transcendent moral foundations.

Economic and personal liberties must be united with the rule of law to nurture loving and just expressions and allow all people to flourish. Objective truths, which guide behavior and relationships, do indeed exist. There must be explicit and implicit values that ensure cohesive and prosperous living. The Holy Spirit gives discernment and wisdom, enabling Christians to engage virtuously in commerce and culture without being enslaved by the perversions of liberty caused by rebellion and sin. Human government is designed to protect God-given (natural) rights, restrain evil, and help steward the public good. Government is subsidiary, exercising its authority and responsibility after personal, familial, religious, and other nearby social institutions flex their proper and more proximate influences. The best policies and practices will only achieve their finest fruit through morally responsible people assuring that this local service is a mark of Christian discipleship. Spirit-empowered churches are crucial for the flourishing of communities and nations. They are God's primary channels of economic, moral, and spiritual good and must not be overtaken by bureaucracies impersonally dispersing largesse.

For Such a Time as This

As the cohesive consensus of Western civilization continues to implode, the time is ripe for a fresh articulation of biblical truth and the virtuous liberties that flow from churches experiencing the presence and power of the Holy Spirit. Pentecostal Christianity is growing exponentially in non-Western nations. The major places of revitalization and transformation in the West are most often led by women and men impacted by Pentecostal/charismatic spirituality. Pope John XXIII called for a "new Pentecost" as Vatican II leaders convened. Evangelical believers are embracing the reality of God's liberating signs of kingdom work. Pentecostals are maturing, aware that no one stream of global Christianity has a "franchise" on the work of the Holy Spirit. The recent (2010) Lausanne meeting in Cape Town acknowledged the deep need for discipleship that integrates spirituality and social transformation without reducing the former to the latter or compromising the full claims of Jesus Christ.

Back-to-the-Future Moments

Church history is replete with examples of discipleship that integrate faith, work, and economics and create flourishing churches and communities. The inspiring stories of these saints will help us appreciate that our efforts matter and that, rather than not inventing something new, we are "catching up" to Jesus and the apostles here in the third millennium.

Revolutionary moments often begin with a humble individual: for example, from St. Benedict's first thoughts on monastic reform to St. Francis's rebuilding of a parish church one stone at a time. Luther wanted to explore ecclesial abuses and Ignatius of Loyola was recovering from the wounds of war. John Wesley did not think souls could be saved outside the church walls until Whitefield called him outdoors. Wilberforce discovered that he didn't need to be a cleric to do God's work. Dorothy Day wanted the poor to eat. William Seymour endured unspeakable prejudice as he listened to Pentecostal thinking from the hallways of a segregated Bible school. Billy Graham knelt on a golf course and surrendered to the authority of Scripture and a call to preach. David du Plessis crossed a raging stream of controversy and attended a World Council of Churches meeting as a Pentecostal. Mother Teresa silenced the voices of her detractors as she discovered the face of Jesus in the discarded babies of Calcutta. Richard John Neuhaus awakened thoughtful Christians to public responsibility. John Stott catalyzed global evangelical preaching, scholarship, and outreach. Today, Pentecostal statesmen such as Peter Kusmic in the Balkans and Ivan Satyavrata in India are leading both theological and sociopolitical renewals.

God uses individuals to spark revival and reformation in every era. Today we may be witnessing something new. Rather than pointing to one individual or movement as the "bonfire" of presence and power, perhaps the Holy Spirit is lighting thousands—

even millions—of "brush fires" as thoughtful Christians find each other, seek the face of God, and respond to the Spirit's call to holy, integrated living that transforms individuals and societies. The synergy of Trinitarian theology, repentant reflection on the state of Christian living, and mutual listening to Scripture, history, and the current wind of the Spirit has the potential to awaken the church and stabilize society. The question for Pentecostals is simple: Are we ready to assume a place of economic and social responsibility without sacrificing the urgency of disciple-making evangelization?

This Work Is for You

As a Pentecostal leader committed to the local church and its mission, you are part of an extraordinary movement that has changed the face of global Christianity. You are also being challenged to see the empowering work of the Spirit apply to every area of life, not just the "spiritual" activities sponsored by the church. In the pages ahead, your vision will be expanded and new possibilities for kingdom service will be explored.

Throughout this work, stories of individual Christians and communities are offered as examples of integrating faith, work, and economics. These narratives—identified as "Profiles in Courage"—include humble workers and well-known magnates. No arena of labor is outside the purview of God's empowering presence. No task is meaningless when kingdom purpose is introduced.

A New Summer Camp

A teenager is filled with the Spirit at the altar during a youth summer camp and feels called to the ministry. Though unable to articulate the details, she knows the Holy Spirit has spoken to her. Her wise youth pastor will fan the flames by helping her discover her gifts, experiment with opportunities to serve, and listen to the Spirit for the best venues of service. Perhaps she will be a pastor or church-planting foreign missionary. The Lord may direct her to the legal or medical profession as part of her calling. If she chooses the route toward ordained ministry, she will still need to be ready to work a "secular job" since most churches can barely support one pastor and many mission fields are closed to visible evangelization.

In the old paradigm, she might get another certificate or degree and be "bivocational" while always waiting for the day she can be "full-time." In the new paradigm proposed in this work, teenagers come to an altar of surrender and ask God to show them how and where they are called to serve.

Our young lady senses pastoral or missionary ministry and is developed and directed as such. She sees her work as part of a larger whole and develops her gifts in relationship to other young adults discovering their vocational domains. One friend goes to nursing school while she is in Bible college. Another friend completes a business degree. They start praying about doing church planting together. Our pastoral leader discovers the transferability of her skills while in Bible college, and when she starts her ministry she is an office manager. She and her professional friends prayerfully consider a location for church planting, work with denominational officials, and begin to reach out.

With the new perspective, the core team meets with business, cultural, educational, and social service leaders to understand the city and region they are serving. They ruminate over matters related to sustainability such as how people will earn a living in the community in the next twenty to forty years. As they launch the church, they decide to arrange the budget to focus on charity, missions, and outreach, with salaries a small percentage of the whole. After two years, our pastor is led to full-time deployment as the team prays and expands its efforts. The exigencies on the ground make this a wise choice.

PROFILE IN COURAGE

Medical Care: Integrating Business and Ministry

Sharon Smith is vice president of a medical device company, responsible for global marketing and sales. Her work requires long hours and much travel. The advances in life-saving technology excite her, and the company is nimble and responsive to markets and trends while anchored in its core mission.

Sharon is also an ordained minister and a missionary-educator, teaching in many Bible colleges in Eastern Europe. She is finishing a doctorate with a focus on an integration of business and ministry that will help pastors and business leaders understand and mutually enrich each other.

For years Sharon has been living the integrated life. She has also experienced dichotomized living and misunderstandings that divide clergy and laity. She is determined to articulate a better way forward for the local and global church. She is an exemplary leader, defying the false gaps that separate lay ministry and sacerdotal responsibility.

A proper view of flourishing is more than legitimizing leadership and labor in the secular realm. A biblical view of economics and work encompasses all domains, from the arts to media, from law to medicine, from agriculture to computer technology, from education to religious leadership. Imagine a church youth group with young men and women filled with the Spirit, biblically trained to share their faith, and excited about the call of God—in whatever field opens up to them!

Honesty about Leadership

Throughout church history, God has called men and women from all backgrounds to serve. Their preparation has been both formal and informal, from shepherds like Amos who disclaimed privilege and title, to regal prophets like Isaiah. Sometimes great leaders are prepared in monasteries, cathedral schools, universities, and seminaries. In Pentecostal fashion, this would be local church Bible institutes, Bible colleges, or seminaries. Other times, God seems to pluck someone out of the world of work and place him or her in a prominent position (think St. Ambrose in fourth-century Milan or some early Methodist preachers on the American frontier or English countryside). We see the same phenomenon today as business leaders feel called and acquire minimal clerical credentials while they bring their charisms and skills to the church or mission agency. We must respect the sovereign Spirit's right to call and use any one in any way. What is more important than formal credentials is character depth, biblical-theological maturity, and the gifts (Rom. 12:4–8) to carry out the calling.

Spiritual leaders do not need to be economic experts or possess exhaustive knowledge of all the fields of their congregants. We must, however, see God's perspectives on work and economics and empower effective service for Christ. And we should learn from God's anointed leaders in all fields of work and strive to integrate their insights into the tapestry of church life.

Getting Started

Sometimes it is good to see the forest from a mountaintop before enjoying a walk through the trees. We begin this adventure toward integration with a panoramic view of the purpose of God in chapter 1. Once we have the big picture in mind, we can delight in unpacking the many gifts offered by Scripture, church history, and contemporary examples of kingdom life. Let's go forward in faith, trusting that the same Lord who called Abram to leave his home and follow divine instructions will also lead us faithfully into the fullness of his will for our churches and communities.

Study Questions

1. What does it mean to honor God with a full day's work?
2. Which of the five guiding principles caught your attention? Why?
3. What is most frustrating and most fulfilling about the life of your local church?
4. What are the economic challenges facing your community and local church?

For Further Reading

Blackard, Gary. *Relevance in the Workplace: Using the Bible to Impact Your Job.* Phoenix: Intermedia Publishing Group, 2011.

Miller, Donald E., and Tetsunao Yamamori. *Global Pentecostalism: The New Face of Social Engagement.* Berkeley: University of California Press, 2007.

Roxburgh, Alan J., and Fred Romanuk. *The Missional Leader: Equipping Your Church to Reach a Changing World.* New York: Jossey-Bass, 2006.

Willard, Dallas. *The Great Omission: Rediscovering Jesus' Essential Teachings on Discipleship.* San Francisco: HarperCollins, 2006.

God's Story | 1

People, Place, and Purpose

When an artist begins a painting, she has a vision for the finished canvas, awash in color and shape, light and shadow, and full of meaning. Yes, sometimes works begin in one direction and the creative process unleashes unexpected brushstrokes, resulting in the finished product being different than the original concept. In either case, great art is created from the inside out, from the wellsprings of experience and imagination, genius and patient work. And when the work is complete, there is a contented (and relieved) sigh as the creator enjoys the fruit of her labor and begins to think about how to display it for the public.

All human analogies about our Creator are imperfect reflections; however, we do worship a divine Artist that created space and time, earth and heaven, physical and spiritual reality. Our almighty, omniscient, omnipotent, omnipresent, infinite-personal triune Lord had a plan "before" all of his creative and redemptive activity that we celebrate in worship and witness. Scripture gives a few poignant glimpses into the counsels of eternity.

All of God's efforts in creation, redemption, and transformation are for "the praise of his glory" (Eph. 1:3–14) and for his "pleasure" (Rev. 4:11 KJV). God's own delight is the first and last purpose of all we see. This is not some kind of ego trip; it is simply noting the reality of God's utter uniqueness: the holiness, love, and unity of his infinite life. "Before the mountains were born or you brought forth the earth and the world, from everlasting to everlasting you are God" (Ps. 90:2).

God did not create out of any lack or need, but out of abundance and joy. God is not "finding himself." Eternal triune life and love intersects with creation, especially the crown jewel of divine artisanship: male and female fashioned in God's image (Gen. 1:26–27; 5:1–2).

God created humankind to enjoy fellowship, to "dwell" with them (Ex. 25, 35; 1 Peter 2:4–10; Rev. 21:1–6) and enjoy reciprocal affection and partnership in caring for creation. The One who is an eternal relation, a divine dance of Father, Son, and Holy Spirit, shares this effervescent love with finite beings, even giving them the option of accepting or rejecting his lordship (2 Peter 3:9).

God's eternal intentions include the reconciling of all creation in Christ (Eph. 1:10; Col. 1:15–22). The focus is a redeemed community from all nations—a people who willingly worship him and carry out his work as a new community of the Spirit (Rev. 4–5).

God delights in putting his redeemed people on display for the rest of creation, like the artist unveiling a canvas for public viewing (Eph. 3:10). The Holy Spirit is actively transforming each believer, and the whole work is compared to a temple, a habitation of holy presence (Eph. 2:19–22).

The concluding words of Jesus' High Priestly Prayer bring eternity and time, intention and fulfillment, together: "Father, I want those you have given me to be with me where I am, and to see my glory, the glory you have given me because you loved me before the creation of the world. . . . I have made you known to them, and will continue to make you known in order that the love you have for me may be in them and that I myself may be in them" (John 17:24, 26).

Creation and History: The Context of God's Plan and the First Layer of the Masterpiece

This eternal plan unfolds in history, with real people in real places fulfilling (or resisting) the divine purpose. The material and spiritual worlds, though distinct, are together part of God's creation and will be part of the eternal kingdom. The material cosmos is not a defect, an imperfection, or a prison that traps the spiritual— it is a good work of the Creator.

Oil paintings known for their brilliant color and light often have an "underpainting" of rich pigments, from neutrals to brilliant reds. On top of this rest the details that we admire. The creation is the "underpainting" of the divine canvas. From God's utterance "Let there be light" to his joyous fashioning of male and female—with the divine commission to multiply, care for the world, and live under God's cultural mandate—the goodness of the "real" world is evident!

The artistry, blessings, and commands of Genesis 1 and 2 remain the will of God for the human family. *Here comes principle one: Work is good!* Before our rebellion and expulsion from Eden, and after the arrival of the fullness of God's kingdom, humans will work because we were designed to be cocreators with God, stewards of the (old and new) earth he created (and will renew). It is vital that we have strong doctrines of creation and anthropology to guide our understanding of discipleship. Being human means that we are physical and spiritual, a "living being" fashioned in God's image—with morality, relational desires, self-awareness, and a will to innovate. All work has meaning, even if the boring and repetitive realities of daily labor sometimes obscure higher purposes. Notice in Genesis 1–3 that humankind enjoyed consistent fellowship with the Lord in a specific place and time (the garden, in the cool of day), marital joy ("one flesh") and purpose in daily life ("Be fruitful and increase in number; fill the earth and subdue it," Gen. 1:28). The one condition was obedience to the divine command.

Alas, sin entered our history through Adam and Eve's primal disobedience, and neither the earth nor humanity has been the same since that awful moment (Rom. 5:12–21; 8:18–25). Here we see *principle two: Sin has effaced but not erased the divine image in humankind, and everyday work still possesses inherent dignity.* With the entry of sin, we see the inauguration of God's eternal redemptive purpose in Christ. From the first promise of Genesis 3:15, where the woman's "seed" or "offspring" (a surprising choice of words in a male-dominated Near Eastern setting!) will "crush the serpent's head," to the final triumphant demonstration of Christ's power as King of kings in Revelation 19–21, the outcome is not in doubt. God will have a people united in worship, enjoying fellowship, and fulfilling their destiny to exercise dominion.

The Old Testament Scriptures offer narration and reflection on the self-disclosure of God's character, nature, and ways and his purposes in electing, commissioning, and refining a people for his glory. The mission of God—God's electing, delivering, covenant-making, and transforming of the nations—takes place in and through people who work and participate in nomadic, agrarian, and urban economies! God's saving activity is not divorced from the economy and the interconnectedness of worship and work: from farmers in Galilee, to shepherds in the Judean hills, to emperors in pagan palaces. Our review of the Old Testament, from David's poetic reflections on divine provision to Nehemiah's urban renewal infused with religious revival and socioeconomic transformation, will unveil these dynamics.

The eternal canvas has a beautiful creation underpainting awash with color. As history moves forward, the painting is defaced with scrawls and tears that threaten the integrity of the canvas and mar the beauty of the final work. But our Redeemer is working to repair the damage and reveal his beauty to the world. Consider these marvelous works of our God through his people:

The election, deliverance, and provision of God for his chosen people Israel;

The revelation through Moses of the moral law, accompanied by angelic glory;

The tabernacle of Exodus is artistry at its finest, with beauty, creativity, generosity, and skill all empowered by the Holy Spirit. This work is one of the repairs to the tears of sin and revelations of divine glory;

Divine interventions throughout Israel's history, from minor judges to major kings, from discipline through defeat to miraculous victories against all odds. We see a sovereign God as the only perfect hero in every narrative. But he accomplished his plans through regular people—all of whom work!

God's final word of self-disclosure, the apex of the story of salvation, is found in the person and work of Jesus Christ. Timeless truth and timely reality perfectly unite in one moment of history: the incarnation (John 1:1–18, especially verse 14). Here we see the brightest and most colorful part of our painting—the words and works of Jesus. *And here is principle three: God has reconciled the world to himself in Christ and is now at work through the church, expressing the life of his eternal kingdom in the present.*

The same biblical pattern of God's saving activity is intensified in Christ:

The church consists of all the believers in Christ who receive
God's offer of grace (Eph. 1:3–14; 1 Peter 1:1–2).

The death and resurrection of Jesus are the saving events that
reach back in time to complete the partial preparation of the
old covenant and then forward in time to touch all the nations through a church going out in mission (Rom. 3:21–31;
2 Cor. 5:14—6:2).

The church is the tabernacle/temple of God (1 Cor. 6:19–20;
2 Cor. 6:16; Eph. 2:19–22; 1 Peter 2:4–10), enjoying the
presence of God the Holy Spirit in each believer and in the
local church.

God is now working through the body of Christ to bring the good
news of forgiveness, deliverance, healing, and hope to all
people; and the world is now beginning to see the peace and
justice of the future invade the present circumstances of
people and entire nations (Matt. 28:18–20; Acts 1:8).

As Spirit-empowered believers live and share the good news, *principle four comes into focus: Compassion and wealth creation are the
overflow of life in the Spirit*, the organic result of believers being
"salt and light" and allowing their good works to glorify God before a watching world (Matt. 5:13–16). Throughout this book,
we will highlight the effect of Christian initiatives in ameliorat-
ing poverty and promoting all forms of abundance (John 10:10).
Christians have always done more than dispense charity! As citizens of the kingdom living the future now in the power of the
Spirit, courageous and thoughtful believers have labored for justice and economic opportunity for two millennia.

The influence of Christianity upon the world is immense;
there is no domain of human activity untouched by the gospel.
There is much for followers of Christ to celebrate. The church is

rightly criticized for some historical mistakes; the balance of the historical record, however, demonstrates the positive impact of the faith on all facets of human life, including work and economics. Christians have led the way in the following:

abolition movements to end all forms of slavery;

establishing fair legal systems;

charitable efforts, especially in caring for the broken, poor, and vulnerable;

affirming the sanctity of every human life, from conception to coronation;

creating environments for entrepreneurs to flourish and to lift the community's economy and welfare;

education expansions and reforms;

intellectual inquiry and the organization and preservation of knowledge;

framing the role of government as subsidiary to church, family, and conscience, yet a partner with other agencies for good;

fostering the arts, including music and visual expressions.

This leads us to *principle five: A flourishing culture, economy, and society must be built on transcendent moral foundations.* This is a way of summarizing the implications of all the "ways of God" found throughout the Bible. Psalm 119 contains 176 verses that all praise the law of the Lord, giving thanks for the breadth and depth, the passion and principles, that are foundational for a God-shaped life.

Spirit-filled believers work hard, participate in the economy, and aim to maximize the impact of the gospel upon all areas of society. But we never lose sight of the fact that all this positive transformation of the whole rests upon transformed individuals who are obedient to the principles of God's Word and sensitive to the Holy Spirit in the application of truth.

As we continue to see God's brushstrokes on the canvas and unpack the implications of discipleship that integrates faith, work, and economics, it is vital for us to avoid two extremes in our efforts to glorify God and bring good to the world. The first extreme is hyperdominionism, in which the world is Christianized completely, before Christ returns, as all the nations come under the theocratic rule of church-approved leaders. The second extreme position is fatalism, a form of hyperdispensationalism that sees no hope for improving current conditions—our only task is to get folks saved and hold on until the rapture.

Jesus left us with a wonderful paradox to keep us dependent upon his power and expectant of his presence. On the one hand, we are to bring the "whole counsel of God" to the whole world, watching the Holy Spirit transform individuals, families, clans, and cultures—even entire nations. On the other hand, Jesus warned us that there will always be rebellion in this present evil age, and the moments before his return in glory will be comparable to the days of Noah (Matt. 24:37–39).

Pentecostals are urgent about evangelism because our Lord is returning soon for his bride! We are also practitioners of kingdom life, bringing deliverance, healing, and reconciliation to the bound, broken, and alienated. As a result of the grace of Christ, local churches are born, communities are changed, and believers begin to take their place as business leaders, advocates for the poor, and educators of the next generation. We can experience the power of the Spirit as we embrace the paradox of evangelistic urgency and responsibility for integrating our faith with all domains of society. It is not an "either/or" venture, but a "both/and" adventure!

PROFILE IN COURAGE

Bob Padgett and Assist International

Bob was a successful Assemblies of God pastor in Santa Cruz, California, leading a missions-minded church of several hundred in a city and county rather hostile to Christianity. In 1989, his direction in life changed as he founded Assist International, a ministry that connects business, humanitarian, and medical professionals with global opportunities for compassion, thus paving the way for gospel impact in otherwise closed or resistant nations.

Assist International has installed cardiac care units in Beijing Children's Hospital; constructed orphanages, dairy farms, and housing in Romania; and stimulated nonprofit and business efforts in multiple nations in the name of Christ. Bob is a Christian leader networking through the Rotary Club International and his contacts with major medical centers in the United States. Here is a Christian pastor deploying "secular" resources for gospel purposes, encouraging education and business, and channeling tens of millions of dollars to people in need.

Bob, his wife, Charlene, and their dedicated team are amazed at the opportunities and resources that have flowed through Assist International in the past two decades. Bob gives all the glory to God and shares how difficult it was to step out in faith like Abraham and start a work that didn't fit any particular "category" at the time.

Assist International is a perfect example of the faith-work-economics integration that is the passion of this book. Yes, the organization is a nonprofit; but their efforts have created flourishing communities with hope for the future. They have fostered wealth creation and resourcefulness in Romania, a land still recovering from the devastations of totalitarianism. They have opened doors for overt Christian work in China by meeting a medical and technological need.

As we adventure forward, let's inquire of God concerning our local congregations and their place of leadership in the revitalization of our communities and of our nation.

Study Questions

1. Do you think much about the "end times"? How do you view your own future in light of what you think about Jesus' imminent return?

2. What ethical/moral principles do you share with most of your non-Christian colleagues and friends? How can these help foster a better future?

3. What are some of the economic and social needs of your community? How can your church be a part of the solution?

4. What are the best and worst parts of the work you do each day?

For Further Reading

Hart, David Bentley. *Atheist Delusions: The Christian Revolution and Its Fashionable Enemies.* New Haven: Yale University Press, 2010.

Hill, Jonathan. *What Has Christianity Ever Done for Us? How It Shaped the Modern World.* Downers Grove, IL: InterVarsity, 2005.

Sheiman, Bruce. *An Atheist Defends Religion: Why Humanity Is Better Off with Religion Than without It.* New York: Alpha, 2009.

Stark, Rodney. *For the Glory of God: How Monotheism Led to Reformations, Science, Witch-Hunts, and the End of Slavery.* Princeton, NJ: Princeton University Press, 2004.

The Story of Creation | 2

Includes the Economy and Work—
Insights from the Old Testament

I n chapter 1, we presented the big picture of God's amazing story. God's activities—his creative, redemptive, and transforming works—take place in the lives of real people who work and participate in the economy. God's plan is not merely a salvage operation, but rather a progressive unfolding to humanity of his character and nature and an invitation to worship and work with God as servants, friends, coworkers, and beloved "spouse."

Christian discipleship must be fully informed by biblical wisdom that unites faith, work, and economics. Neither the ancient Israelites nor the New Testament Christians would have separated the "practical" and the "spiritual" or the "personal" and the "social," as so many do today. From Genesis to Revelation, the Bible has much to say about economics and work. The wisdom we distill from Scripture is vital if we are going to have flourishing churches and communities.

In this chapter we will examine the straightforward teaching of Scripture concerning economics and work. We must acknowledge that sinful humanity has selectively abused various texts of the Bible to serve selfish ideological, material, and political purposes. As we begin this part of the story, here are some qualifiers so that we can focus on clear principles:

⬦ *A biblical perspective has no place for greed, crass materialism, or a facile prosperity ideology that reduces divine favor to economic or social status.*

⬦ *In a fallen but beginning-to-be-redeemed world, there will be economic disparities.* Some of these are due to personal sin. Other factors include natural events, geographical/resource factors, oppressive rulers, systemic dysfunction, and ideological/religious captivity that suppress God-given abilities and opportunities.

⬦ *Economics and work are not all of life.* They are integral to a healthy life, but not the total picture. Properly understood, a robust view of economics and work will propel progress in all dimensions, from the creative arts to educational reform to political freedom.

⬦ *The Bible offers sufficient foundations for wise stewardship, but it does not offer all the information we need for contemporary flourishing.* It is right to look at the common grace of empirical observation and research. We then subject our findings to biblical principles and prayerful reflection on the Spirit's activity in our context.

⬦ *Though God's principles are universal, the particularities of location, history, and resources will yield unique results.* We must avoid a cookie-cutter approach to discipleship, both in our personal lives and in our communities. God is fashioning each believer and every local church as unique works of art. The song of the redeemed in the coming kingdom will be a symphony of diverse colors, languages, and movements we can all enjoy and understand.

With these thoughts in mind, let's take a journey through Scripture, distilling clear principles for our twenty-first-century lives.

The Call to Work: Genesis 1–11; Exodus 20:9; Deuteronomy 5:13; Psalms 8; 19:1–6

Humankind is the crown of God's creation, the final formative act in the creative week that begins with light and ends with joyous rest. The narratives of Genesis 1 and 2 reveal a sovereign God distinct from his creation yet engaged with space and time and intimately present with our first parents. The poetry of Genesis 1:26–27; 2:22–25; and 5:1–2 unveils several things about God's intentions for humankind:

- ⟡ Humankind—male and female—uniquely bears the image of God and is endowed with moral, relational, and spiritual faculties consistent with the divine likeness.

- ⟡ The call to steward God's creation—to tend the garden— antedates the tragedy of sin. In other words, we are made to work, and caring for creation is good.

- ⟡ The physical world, the real world of work and play, labor and rest, is good. The material world, as made by God, is not a result of disaster nor is it disconnected from spiritual realities. As designed and declared by God, creation is good.

- ⟡ The labor ordained for humankind was not the only activity of life. Implicit in Genesis 1–10 and Psalm 8 are broader mandates to enjoy the presence of God (who "walks" in the garden on a daily basis), marry and have children, cultivate the arts and technology, and find time to rest and reflect on the seventh day.

Alas, the entrance of sin in Genesis 3 ruins this bucolic portrait of purpose and relationship. Intimacy with God is marred by fear, marital relations are subverted by selfishness, and labor becomes a quest for surviving instead of thriving. From Genesis 3–11 we observe the consequences of sin: murder is celebrated (4:23–24); immorality is rampant (6:1–5); and self-worship attempts to displace the divine (11:1–4). It is important in the midst of these sorrowful narratives to assert what is *not* said. *Here again we see principle two at work: God's image is effaced but not erased in fallen humankind.* Psalm 8 reminds people of their inherent dignity, even with the depravity that subverts divine intentions. Sinners are capable of accepting or rejecting God's grace.

Work may be laborious and less fruitful, but it is still what we are made to do. There is a danger in thinking that prefall humanity lived in a vacation paradise punctuated with occasional plucking of fruit from the trees. We are made to be cocreators with God, resting one day in seven and finding purpose in all we do.

Sin is a perversion of the good. Spurred on by the devil, sin cannot create anything—it can only twist the good into something evil, from sexual intimacy to labor to family relationships.

In the book of Revelation, eternal life is embodied existence, worshipful and working as God dwells with humankind and the redeemed realize their full purpose (Rev. 7; 11; 21–22). The nations scattered in judgment (Gen. 10–11) are now gathered in feasting (Rev. 19). The covenant of marriage honored in Genesis 2 reaches its spiritual fulfillment as God the Father presents a perfect bride (purified by the power of the Holy Spirit) to God the Son.

A review of select scriptural narratives reveals a loving, purposeful, and reconciling Lord, reaching out to humankind and unveiling meaning to all aspects of life.

Election for Universal Blessing:
Genesis 12–22; Exodus 1–20

God's election of Abraham (Gen. 12:1–3; 15) and his descendants through Isaac (Gen. 18; 21–22), culminating in the consecration of the nation of Israel (Ex. 3–20), is a dramatic narrative misunderstood by many. *God chose Abraham and Israel in order to bless the whole world, not to foster elitism among one ethno-religious group. It is imperative that the particularity of God's election be positioned within God's desire to embrace and reconcile all humankind.* God does have the sovereign right to choose his servants in salvation history (Rom. 9–11); however, election carries responsibilities as well as privileges—and the biblical narratives are full of the divine discipline of God's people (Deut. 32)!

The story of Israel is a paradigm of the gracious work of God that will reach its fulfillment in the coming of Christ. Discipleship takes place in relationship with a covenant-keeping God who delights in steadfast love (*hesed*). Notice the order of events that lead to the establishment of Israel, and the parallels with the work of Christ.

First, we see God's *election* as he chooses to show grace to the undeserving (Gen. 12; Ex. 3–4; Deut. 1–4). God did not choose Abraham or Israel because they were better, greater in number, or more powerful than other nations. God graciously adopted his people, period. In John 15 and Ephesians 1 we see that believers are graciously chosen in Christ and ordained to fruitful work in the world.

Second, God supernaturally *delivers* his people from oppression (Ex. 13–15) and provides for all their needs, despite their forgetfulness and rebellion (Ex. 16–17). Paul teaches in Romans 3:9—5:21 that God's merciful work of salvation through the atoning death of Christ is completely gracious and prior to any spiritual inclinations on our part.

Third, God *makes a covenant* with the nation, setting them apart as royal priests, with a calling to worship and witness (Exodus 19:6 is perhaps the greatest verse in the Torah). At the Last Supper and in Paul's eucharistic retelling of Jesus' words and works, a new covenant of grace through the blood of Christ is declared (Luke 22 and 1 Cor. 10–11).

After electing, delivering, and covenant-making, *the Lord reveals the ten words (Ten Commandments, Ex. 20; cf. Deut. 5) to Moses, declaring the moral-relational character of the Almighty and the pathway to fulfillment.* Likewise, all Christian service is a "thank-you" to God for the undeserved kindness shown in Christ (Eph. 4:1; Col. 3:1–3).

The biblical order forever ends the notion that the Old Testament is just "law" and the New Testament is "grace." All of God's creative and redemptive activities are gracious and direct us toward covenant love. There is continuity between the testaments! Christ has fulfilled the law (Heb. 5–10) and the Holy Spirit indwells all Christians (1 Cor. 6:19); however, covenantal love from Genesis to Revelation is gracious and is never the consequence of human effort.

Anointed Artisans: Exodus 25; 35–36

The first major activity God directs for his redeemed people on their way to the promised land is a community art project called the tabernacle. God instructs Moses to build a beautiful but portable dwelling that will signify the manifest presence of the glory of God. The first "filling with the Spirit" is bestowed upon Bezalel (Ex. 35:31), the chief artisan of the furnishings of worship.

It is interesting that this project is the only time that God's people were told to stop giving (Ex. 36:2–7)! The response was overwhelming, as gratitude begat generosity. *Maybe the giving in your local church will be more cheerful and generous if the congregants can connect their offerings with relational and tangible progress in kingdom goals that they are part of discovering and implementing.*

By the way, "The poor need beauty as well as bread" (Ray Bakke). It is not too expensive to invite artists and artisans, builders and craftsmen, to adorn the worship locale with color, light, and images that convey the mission, vision, and values of the community. Simplicity does not mean plainness, and good stewardship includes aesthetic leadership.

Liberated for Stewardship

The books of Exodus, Leviticus, Numbers, and Deuteronomy are filled with moral, ceremonial, and civil legislation, all designed to foster harmony and justice. There is much that is instructive for the domains of worship and work, as well as personal and community life. Christians do debate about the imperatives of the Old Testament and their application to an international community of the Holy Spirit. Hebrews makes it clear that the sacrifice of Christ and his triumph over death fulfills and replaces the ceremonial legislation of the old covenant. It is equally clear that the moral teachings of the Torah are continued and even intensified in the New Testament. Jesus' ethical teaching reiterates the prophetic priorities of the Hebrew Scriptures (Matt. 5–7; Luke 6). There is no room for compromise or "cheap grace."

The application of the Old Testament civil case laws and the ordinances governing money, property, and punitive rules for criminal behavior are hotly debated among serious Bible students, but the ethical imperatives are lasting. Politically conservative Christians find the foundations for legislation in the laws of Israel, especially for property rights and moral conduct. Christians of more liberal persuasion focus on the Sabbath and Jubilee narratives, arguing for greater care for the poor and more equitable distribution of wealth.

It is possible to transcend ideological preferences and find some important principles for our lives, all of which are explicitly or implicitly continued in the new covenant community:

✧ All laws are built on a foundation of transcendent morality that represents the character and commands of God. (Here we see principle five at work.) Freedom cannot exist without virtue, and real liberty requires the rule of law. *There is no separation of private morality from the public good.*

✧ Personal property rights and the welfare of the community are equally important. The poor are cared for through mandated activities (gleaning and offerings), while hard work and prosperity are celebrated.

✧ Life may bring difficult economic times for some, even temporary loss of land and full economic freedoms; such a low estate is not permanent for successive generations, however (Lev. 25).

✧ *The vulnerable are objects of God's love and the care of his people.* Aliens, orphans, and widows deserve support, first from family and then from the community of faith (Ruth 1–4).

The history of Israel is not a narrative of righteous practice, but one of backsliding, judgment, and repentance/restoration (see especially the book of Judges). The Torah is instructive for its combination of clarity and mercy. God's people are the chosen—and the demands of God's covenant are stringent. The Lord explains that his commands are given for the ultimate good of each person and the nation (Deut. 10:12–13).

The story of Nehemiah is helpful in observing how the law was implemented on the ground hundreds of years later. This anointed leader demanded that every family care for their personal property as well as help rebuild the city walls (Neh. 3–4). He enforced the principles against usury and compelled the rich to stop unjustly oppressing the poor (Neh. 5). With Ezra, he led revivals in hearing and obeying God's Word as well as in celebrating the goodness of the Lord (Neh. 8). There is no need to over-spiritualize this narrative. The moral, religious, and social integration in this moment of history is an excellent example of discipleship integration among the people of God.

Covenant Enforcement

The prophets of Israel—from Moses and Samuel to Elijah and Elisha, from the stern visions of Joel to the covenant cries of Hosea—were not aiming to be creative theologians or predictors of the future. They were first and foremost heralds of repentance, "covenant enforcers" calling God's people back to fidelity before the Lord and with each other. The prophets identified three interconnected concerns that are vital in any era, especially in the amoral ethos of much of the twenty-first century:

Idolatry

To serve and worship any entity but the Lord God is the core problem of humankind, whether we are chasing fertility deities (1 Kings 18–19; Hosea) or falling headlong into personal and social reprobation through rebellion (Rom. 1:18–32). The deceptive thing about idolatry is that many are not aware of the subtle syncretism that creeps into the human soul. Syncretism is combining one or more gods and religious systems. There is no place for this in biblical faith (Ex. 20:1-6; 1 John 5:21).

The ancient Israelites believed in the Lord God—yet many of them cut deals with local fertility gods in the hope of a good crop and in order to enjoy sexual license under the guise of religious practice. Modern Christians try to live a "Jesus and . . ." life: Jesus and New Age self-help, Jesus and Buddhist meditation, Jesus and materialism, etc. The most heinous syncretism of all is found among theologians who believe it is their duty to "update" Christianity with contemporary thought that wipes away the outdated, narrow beliefs and behaviors enjoined by biblical writers in favor of more enlightened and informed thinking. Such arrogance displaces these thinkers from the global-historical body of Christ.

Immorality

When the Lord God is not exclusively worshiped and obeyed, changes in ethical behavior are not far behind. Self-indulgence in food, money, sex, and power were all part of the other religious systems surrounding Israel. Hosea's message is especially poignant, as the Lord tearfully asks his people (like a spouse pleading with a wayward partner), "What have I done?" God delivered, provided for, disciplined, and restored his people over and over again—but yet was rewarded with spiritual and physical adultery.

Injustice

When syncretism subverts worship and morals are "relaxed," serious legal and social problems will ensue. It is interesting that Amos exposes the corruption of the legal system as a primary consequence of departure from covenant fidelity. If one can craft his or her own deity and moral structure, then legal and social justice default to the highest bidder! Practically speaking, most people who go to court would rather have a high-priced attorney than a public defender. George Orwell's dictum is proven daily in courts across the world:

"Some people are more equal than others." Beyond courtroom dramas, injustice unveils its miserable self in varied ways. Athletes who insist on "renegotiating" multiyear contracts, petty tyrants in city hall who prevent reasonable development with endless fees and hearings, and investment professionals who squander the life savings of working-class people are all in need of repentance.

Pentecostal Christians share the prophets' deep concerns for fidelity to God and for personal morality. In recent decades we have started to reflect on the public justice issues that flow from infidelity to God. There is no place for a facile "prosperity gospel" that treats God like some kind of heavenly vending machine (insert the right prayers and confessions, along with an offering for your favorite television persona, and out comes material wealth). God *does* answer prayers and prosper people; biblical truth, however, must "apply equally in Albania and Alabama" (Gordon Fee). Faith for miraculous interventions needs to grow. But such faith must be tempered by the wisdom that is a gift from the same God who performs the miracles.

Concrete Wisdom for Daily Life

Each of the poetic or wisdom books of the Hebrew Scriptures is concerned with knowledge gained from experience.

Job: Faith when the Formulas Fail

Modern Christians in the West are awash with formulaic self-help books, both Christian and secular. "Five . . . Ten . . . Ninety-nine Steps to . . ." fill the shelves. While some of the advice is biblical (or, at least, a part of natural revelation), the formulaic mindset of these works creates crises of faith when life intrudes with tragedy and unforeseen circumstances.

The drama of Job is helpful for understanding that we are in a real spiritual battle (2 Cor. 10:1–6; Eph. 6:10–20). Though we dare not blame every difficulty on demons, some circumstances are much more than mere misfortune.

This does not mean that purity of faith and obedience to God are fruitless. God commended Job and ultimately restored him. *The question for the serious follower of Christ is whether we will endure hardship for a greater reward or fall away because life is unexplainably hard.*

The experience of Job finds its ultimate fulfillment in Christ's agonizing cry of "*Lama* [Why]?" (Matt. 27:46) as he suffers alienation and the full wrath of God for humankind's sins (Rom. 3:21–26; 2 Cor. 5:18–21). In the unspeakable and unexplainable mystery of his passion, Jesus bears the weight of all human sorrow, carrying the collective "Why?" of undeserved suffering, thus forever identifying with the battered child, genocide victim, and all victims of injustice.

The Psalms: Complaint and Praise— Sometimes in the Same Moment!

The Psalter is the hymnbook of Israel and the church and remains the source for most contemporary expressions of worship. The observations, testimonies, and liturgies of this Davidic-inspired collection are moving and transforming for all who engage them fully. The Psalms offer instruction to whole-life disciples, including the following:

⬧ God is worthy of worship at all times in all circumstances. As Creator, Savior, and Sovereign, he is Lord over the cosmos and the nations, over all the powers arrayed against the righteous, and he will have the final word (Pss. 90–100).

✧ It is good to bring our sorrows to God, personally and collectively, and receive comfort and perspective while we await divine intervention (Pss. 42–43; 73).

✧ It is important to testify of God's goodness and celebrate answers to prayers and victories in trials (Pss. 32; 116).

As a leader of your faith community, encourage your members to pray, sing, and memorize these songs from the heart. Biblical and historical testimony, as well as recent educational research, demonstrate that memorizing Scripture will enhance spiritual growth (Pss. 1; 119). Faith will deepen, wisdom will grow, and strength will be found in the middle of boardroom contention or parent-teacher conflicts. Humility grows when we compare our character to the Almighty. Self-worth develops in a healthy way as we ponder the exalted status of human beings (Ps. 8).

Proverbial Wisdom: Reflections on Reality

An important interpretive lesson from Proverbs for followers of Christ is not to treat these inspired observations as legal decrees. Just because a child is raised well does not mean she or he will automatically reconcile with the church before death (Prov. 22:6). All things considered, the fear of the Lord and diligent labor bring better consequences (Prov. 2–5), but they do not exempt the righteous from suffering. There are sound precepts for stewarding talent and wealth, but no guarantees of untold riches. Here are some of the key ideas throughout this collection of inspired observations:

The fear of the Lord (reverential awe that recognizes his perfection and sovereignty) is the foundation of true knowledge, wisdom, and understanding and the key that unlocks divine guidance and favor (Prov. 1:1–7).

Wisdom in all aspects of life, including economics and work, is offered to the diligent seeker (2:1–22) who comes to God with trust and humility (3:1–6) and a pure heart (4:23–27).

Diligence at work is crucial for prosperity that provides for one's family and releases resources for others (Prov. 6:6–11; 10:4; 12:24, 27; 13:4; 14:23; 19:15). There is no place for laziness in the service of the Lord.

Honesty and integrity in economic affairs are of paramount importance. Good accounting practices, paying workers their due in a timely fashion, and gaining wealth legitimately are commended. Conversely, covert and overt thievery through bribery and dishonest communication incurs the judgment of the Almighty, who is always looking out for the poor (10:2; 11:1; 13:11; 20:10; 23:10–11).

God is more concerned with *holy and mature character* than the size of the bank account (11:4, 28; 15:16–17; 23:4–5).

Accumulated wealth should be wisely managed, and generosity that seeks the glory of God and the good of neighbor is commendable before God (11:24–25; 14:21, 31; 22:9; 28:27).

When good people prosper and public officials are honest with resources, there is joy and provision for all (11:10–11). *Personal success contributes to the welfare of all.*

Hebrew wisdom is concrete, moral, and practical, eschewing esoteric speculation in favor of relational fidelity with the Lord and loving justice toward humankind, especially the needy. Proverbs needs to be part of the daily diet, reminding Christians that practical work in the world brings honor to God and good to the community.

As we encourage our congregations, let's open their minds to involvement in education, conservation, business zoning, social services, community outreach, and chamber of commerce leadership. There is biblical insight for all these activities. Jesus does not fit into neat ideological or politically narrow boxes. About the time individualism begins to rule, caring for one another intrudes on our self-absorbed soliloquies. As C. S. Lewis famously communicates in *The Chronicles of Narnia*, Jesus is "not a tame lion." He is too compassionate for rigid conservatives and too morally demanding for lazy liberals. The key for Christians is to ask how the Bible and the historical and contemporary work of the Holy Spirit inform engagement in these arenas.

Ecclesiastes: Where *Not* to Find Meaning

Derek Kidner, commenting on the gloomy perspective of the author of Ecclesiastes, summarizes the message of this enigmatic book: "Life does not hold the clue to itself." The Teacher looks for meaning in work, pleasure, and learning, finding only emptiness— until he returns to the fear of the Lord and the awareness that there is more to life than what our minds imagine or our senses process (Eccl. 1–4; 12).

Let's note that play and work, friendship and marriage, though not the final ends of life, are good. Once again, *the Hebraic concreteness of life is on display, in radical contrast to other philosophies and religions that eschew the physical world as illusory or evil.*

This is a great book to foster an eternal, untransitory perspective. We will stand before God, who will bring all secrets to light and scrutinize the service of Christ-followers (1 Cor. 3:12–15; 2 Cor. 5:9–10). Full engagement in all spheres of life must be balanced by awareness of the temporal nature of all human constructs.

"God Wrote It First"—
Lessons from the Old Testament

One day Richard Israel, an Old Testament scholar and religion professor at Vanguard University, was asked why he chose to study the Old Testament when "everyone knows that Christians are New Testament people." Professor Israel kindly replied, "I study the Old Testament because God wrote it first. It was also the holy Scripture that Paul told Timothy to read and in which salvation in Christ is found. God's people were a people of the book before they possessed the land. The church affirms that the Old Testament is authoritative and inspired, so I guess we ought to know it well."

There are many interpretive issues that inform how Christians read and apply the Old Testament. Pentecostals have always found rich meaning in the dramatic narratives of God's heroic activity, as well as principles for life and mission in the prophetic and wisdom literature. For discipleship in light of the finished work of Christ and the empowering presence of the Holy Spirit, several insights inform New Testament living. Here are just a few as we prepare to examine the impact of Christ and his inauguration of the reign of God:

Creation is the good work of a holy, loving, transcendent Lord who called forth the cosmos *ex nihilo* by his word and Spirit (Ps. 33:6; cf. Heb. 11:1–6).

Principle one is reaffirmed: Humanity uniquely bears the image of God. Men and women are called to be stewards of the earth, filling it with descendants and the fruit of their labors (Gen. 1–2; 5; cf. James 3:9).

Principle two again: The fall devastated all relationships, but the image of God remains and the call to work has never been withdrawn. The Sabbath is woven into creation and redemption and reminds us to trust God to provide in six days what we need for seven (Ex. 20:8–11; Deut. 5:12–15; cf. Mark 2:27).

Principle four in brief: The overarching biblical narrative is not the human quest for God but God's desire to reconcile a race of rebels. The election of Israel and the church are not exclusionary but gracious, inviting God's people to partner in redeeming the world (Isa. 49; 61; cf. Acts 1:8; 2 Cor. 5:14—6:2).

Principle five: Israel's moral laws, especially the Ten Commandments, remain in force for the people of God, including the motives behind all actions (Jer. 7; Mic. 6; cf. Matt. 5).

God cares about every domain of life, including community worship, family harmony, ethical work, caring for the poor, and establishing a just society (Lev. 18–25; Deut. 1–11; cf. James 3–5).

Salvation is the gracious work of God, and no one can claim any credit for God's sovereign love. The only response to the covenantal love of God is fidelity that is a heartfelt thank-you for divine mercy (Pss. 16; 116; Jonah 2:9; cf. Eph. 4:1).

When God's Word is obeyed, there are positive personal, familial, social, and political effects (Deut. 28; cf. 1 Tim. 2:1–8).

This is robust living with a seamless integration of Sabbath worship, hard work, family health, and social responsibility—all in anticipation of the kingdom of God yet to come.

In the Hebrew Scriptures that honor the Creator we also find maxims that can guide our thinking on the economy and work. Remember the goal of this effort: the integration of faith, work, and economics. We have just started the journey! *It is important at this juncture to stress that the mission of God, the Great Commission of the church, the eternal purpose of the Trinity, takes place in and through people who wake up every day and work, participating in the larger economy, either adding or extracting value from the world. Here is principle four in action.*

As we approach the fullness of God's reconciling work through Jesus Christ, it is wise to consider that our Lord was Jewish, deeply rooted in the Scriptures, and his words and works will affirm the lasting principles as well as provide context for the facets of the Old Testament that are now fulfilled in the new covenant. Augustine's dictum is helpful here: "The New is in the Old concealed; the Old is in the New revealed." Jesus Christ is the final word of salvation—he is the full disclosure of our infinite-personal God who passionately loves us and is determined to dwell with us!

Study Questions

1. What is your calling? How does it relate to the work you do every day? (Note: Don't worry if your answer isn't profound and theological!)

2. What are some financial principles that govern your family life and the life of your congregation? Where are they found in Scripture?

3. What does "fair" mean to you in the world of economics, taxes, and work? How do your notions of fairness align with the Bible passages mentioned here?

4. How does your work contribute to the local community and economy?

For Further Reading

Attanasi, Katherine, and Amos Yong, eds. *Pentecostalism and Prosperity.* New York: Palgrave-Macmillan, 2012.

Corbett, Steve, and Brian Fikkert. *When Helping Hurts: How to Alleviate Poverty without Hurting the Poor . . . and Yourself.* 2nd ed. Chicago: Moody, 2012.

Kidner, Derek. *The Message of Ecclesiastes* (Bible Speaks Today). Downers Grove, IL: IVP Academic, 2004.

Sowell, Thomas. *Economic Facts and Fallacies.* New York: Basic, 2008.

Stearns, Richard. *The Hole in the Gospel.* Nashville: Thomas Nelson, 2010.

The Story of Redemption | 3

Living the Future Now—
Insights from the New Testament

"The color line was washed away through the blood of Jesus Christ. . . . Men and women went from Azusa Street empowered to witness. Some bought one-way tickets to a foreign land. The urgency of the hour was so strong that all notions of denominational structures or religious institutions were swept away in an urgency to complete the Great Commission in light of the imminent return of Jesus Christ."

Cecil M. Robeck Jr.,
The Azusa Street Mission and Revival

"Jesus is risen, therefore God's new world has begun. Jesus is risen, therefore his followers have a new job to do (always imperfectly, until Jesus comes) . . . to bring the life of heaven in actual, physical, earthly reality. Every act of love, every deed done in Christ and by the Spirit, every work of true creativity—doing justice, making peace, healing families, resisting temptation, seeking and winning true freedom—is an earthly event in a long history of things that implement Jesus' own resurrection and anticipate the final new creation and act as signposts of hope, pointing back to the first and on to the second."

N. T. Wright, *Surprised by Hope*

The New Testament: Continuity, Fulfillment, and Transformation

As we turn to the New Testament, we discover much continuity as well as some contrasts with the Hebrew Scriptures. The contrasts are mostly connected with an expansion of fellowship to all nations and the fulfillment of ceremonial/sacrificial obligations in light of the work of Christ. *The continuities are much greater in number, and we find liberation for all the nations in the new covenant in Christ. The missional God who called Abraham has empowered all of his people to share the good news in word and work with all people.*

As the time for Christ draws near (Mark 1:1–8; Gal. 4:4–5), expectations for spiritual renewal are united with the hope of a new king, David, who will destroy the political and spiritual enemies of God and establish a lasting reign of peace and justice (Isa. 2; Mic. 4; Mal. 3–4).

John the Baptist: Anointed Forerunner and a Preview of the Kingdom

In Matthew 11 Jesus declares that John the Baptist is the greatest prophet of all time and the forerunner of his messianic ministry. John called Israel to repentance in expectation of the coming of the kingdom in Christ (Matt. 3; Mark 1; Luke 3; John 1; 3).

For this work, the ethical implications of true repentance seen in Luke 3:10–14 reveal principles that apply to the people of God in all times and places. As humble listeners respond to his calls to holiness, they inquire about the actions that must flow from a changed heart. John tells them that they should share with the poor (generosity), collect only the proper imperial taxes (no extra cut for tax collectors, so be people of integrity), and be content with their wages by refraining from extortion and intimidation (soldiers are to protect, not exploit).

What makes this passage instructive for faith, work, and economics is the ethics that transform personal and institutional behavior and the prophetic role Christians can play in the economic and social life of the world:

- ✧ Heartfelt generosity is a virtue of any serious believer;

- ✧ Integrity in financial affairs is the norm;

- ✧ Contentment without covetousness is vital for divine approbation.

For John the Baptist, Jesus of Nazareth, and all subsequent Christian teaching, love means action. Sacrificial care for others is the heart of the gospel-in-action. As we continue to learn about faith, work, and economics, the call of John the Baptist to prove our repentance by serving others with no thought of return is foundational to Christian life and divine favor.

The Presence of the Future: The Kingdom of God in the Words and Works of Jesus

All four gospels communicate the reality that the coming of Jesus is "fulfillment awaiting consummation" (Herman Ridderbos), with God's reign breaking into history in the words and works of Christ. Jesus' powerful teaching ("with authority," unlike his pedantic rivals—Matt. 7:28–29) and miraculous signs awakened messianic expectations and caused the crowd to agitate for immediate political change (John 6:14–15).

Jesus announced the paradoxical presence of the kingdom of God (Mark 1:14–15; Luke 4:16-21; 17:20–21), affirming the present reality of deliverance, forgiveness, healing, and reconciliation while calling on his followers to remain faithful until his return in glory. Even after his bodily resurrection and appearances, some followers were still asking about an immediate, visible reign. Jesus leaves the timing of the final day of the Lord to the Father and commands his followers to prepare for their global mission by waiting for the Holy Spirit's empowerment (Acts 1:1–11).

John reminds believers that all the signs and teachings of Jesus cannot be contained in books (John 21:25). All of the "red letters" apply to Christian discipleship, but for the purpose of integration here are some insights that guide our kingdom stewardship:

- ✧ *Jesus' experience of the power of the Holy Spirit is the pattern for the Christian life.*

  Jesus was conceived in Mary's womb by the overshadowing work of the Spirit (Luke 1:26–38). This same sovereign Spirit regenerates the soul in conversion (John 3:3–8).

  Jesus was anointed for his public messianic mission at his baptism, with the manifest presence of the Spirit and the voice of the Father affirming his special status. On the day of Pentecost, and in subsequent moments of grace, God's people (already regenerated—John 20:19–22) are anointed for mission, and signs and wonders accompany the proclamation of the gospel.

  Jesus submitted to the leading of the Spirit. Sometimes this meant going into the wilderness or other obscure places. These occasions often became divine appointments. In all his works, he sought only the will of the Father (Matt. 4; John 4; 5; 8; 10). All Christians live by the Spirit and can learn to keep in step with the Spirit, personally and in community (Gal. 5:16–26).

Jesus' death and resurrection secured the salvation of all who believe. No one forced him to travel the pathway of agony and alienation, but for the joy set before him (our reconciliation) he endured the cross and was vindicated on Easter morning (John 2; 5; 8; 17; Rom. 5; Heb. 9; 12:2; cf. Isa. 52–53). Christians are called to walk in his steps, enduring persecution for the gospel and fellowshipping with the passion and resurrection of the Lord (Phil. 3:10–11; 1 Peter 2:21).

✧ *As the people of the Spirit, we can expect miraculous signs to accompany our outreach.* Perhaps the absence of exorcisms, healings, and other miracles is not because of divine reluctance, but rather because of our own insular spirituality that waits for the lost to find our buildings and programs. John Wimber, founder of the Vineyard fellowship of churches, reminded the world that power accompanies evangelism and that miracles are not simply for entertainment within carefully crafted religious programming. Brett and Lyn Johnson's rep business/mission efforts demonstrate that God does the miraculous in boardrooms and on factory floors, in fields and in homes.

✧ *Living the future now in the power of the Spirit embraces the call of Christ to die and live, lose to gain, become lowly to be exalted by God, leave all and follow—and discover our deepest longings fulfilled!* There is a general truth here: all Christians must be obedient to the precepts of Scripture. There is also particularity to the leading of the Spirit: some leave their fishing business and become full-time apostolic emissaries; others are enjoined to be about their daily tasks as they wait for the Lord's coming. If material wealth is one's deity, abandonment may be the only way to salvation, while others will gain abundant wealth in the service of God. Each Christian must ask, "Is Christ really Lord? If he is, then where could I serve him best?"

✧ *There is urgency and realism about the future.* At any moment, life can end with an accounting demanded by the Lord (Luke 12:20; Heb. 9:27–28). The visible arrival of the Lord and the full establishment of the kingdom will come on the appointed day; meanwhile, believers must be about the Great Command and the Great Commission, occupying their assigned posts until the Master arrives (Matt. 24:36–51; Acts 1:6–8). "Being about the Lord's business" includes business and commerce, education and social work, evangelization and all other God-ordained facets of human living.

Those who aspire to be "red-letter people" must consider the fact that the red letters not only contain words of compassion, unconditional love, and denunciation of materialism and power-seeking (Luke 6:20–36). The red letters also call for moral purity from the inside out, marital fidelity, hard work, and awareness of impending judgment and grace as Christ returns (Matt. 5–7; 19; 23–25). Jesus cannot be constrained by any ideological straitjackets.

The Holy Spirit Changes Everything:
Personal and Social Transformation in Acts

The gospel of Luke and the book of Acts are not mere narratives. They represent accurate history, missionary apologetics, and theological reflection—all in the context of the work of the Holy Spirit. Pentecostals are intuitive narrative theologians, believing that doctrine and practice are found in the Gospels and Acts as well as the Epistles. The publication of I. H. Marshall's *Luke: Historian and Theologian* in 1979 and Roger Stronstad's *The Charismatic Theology of St. Luke* in 1984 (which was expanded in 2012) are part of an academic awakening promoting the thesis that the Holy Spirit inspired the shaping of Luke-Acts so that it yields important insights into normative Christian discipleship.

Jesus commissions and empowers his early followers in Luke 10 and rejoices when they return with testimonies of deliverance and impact. As the risen Lord, he instructs his followers to wait in Jerusalem for the outpouring of the Spirit that will enable them to fulfill their global mission (Luke 24:44–49; Acts 1:4–8).

The enflamed believers of Acts 2:1–4 are the engaged followers of Acts 2:42–47. Being filled with the Spirit means enthusiasm for witness and overflowing love for all people. We will unpack the principles of Luke-Acts in greater detail. Enthusiasm for the liveliness of the first-century church must be tempered with realism about the context of some events. Biblical descriptions are not always prescriptions, and we must not try to superficially recreate the ancient church, even while being utterly faithful to the apostolic gospel. The stories in Acts inform our missionary outreach, fellowship, leadership, and theology—and God accomplished all his works through people who worked for a living!

In his book *The King Jesus Gospel*, Scot McKnight unites a scholar's eye and a passion for discipleship as he surveys the narratives and speeches in Acts. McKnight affirms that the apostolic preaching of the early church called people to a total change of allegiance through repentance and faith. The weakness of the contemporary church is a failure to unite Jesus' gracious atoning work on the cross (Rom. 3:21–31; 2 Cor. 5:18–21) with the radical call to follow Christ at all costs (Luke 9:23–25).

In the book of Acts we see the new community learning to live together in faith, hope, and love as they are transformed by the teachings of Jesus and the apostles. And we observe the following amazing developments as a result of the coming of the Spirit:

✧ All believers are empowered—not just a priestly elite. The work of the Spirit engenders community prayer and hospitality (Acts 2:42–47).

✧ The Holy Spirit cares about practical needs, and anointed leaders are appointed to care for widows (Acts 6:1–7).

✧ All are welcome into the "incendiary fellowship" (as D. Elton Trueblood titled the book he wrote in 1978) of the Spirit-empowered community—including Samaritans (mortal enemies of the Jews) and Gentiles (Acts 8; 10).

✧ God chose to use Saul/Paul, the most Jewish of Jews, to expand his mission to the Gentiles (Acts 9; 11; 13–28). At the same time, new converts need to show their gratitude for such grace and help their starving sisters and brothers (2 Cor. 8–9; cf. 1 John 2–3).

✧ The first church council in AD 49 affirmed the inclusion of non-Jews, with a few moral and practical provisos to engender fellowship (Acts 15). It is also important to note that Jews did not need to cease their specific practices of diet and Sabbath-keeping in order to be a part of the messianic community.

✧ The church in Europe begins in the home of a wealthy businesswoman (Acts 16:6–15).

✧ When the Spirit is working, there will be spiritual, political, and socioeconomic warfare as truth confronts deception (Acts 18–19).

The New Testament epistles are ad hoc documents (with the possible exception of Paul's "letter of introduction" to the Romans and his circular letter to the Ephesians) written by the apostles to answer queries, resolve conflicts, and address moral and spiritual issues of concern. The insights are numerous, and the clear moral and theological assertions have directed Christian living for two millennia. For the integration we envision, let's consider the following:

✧ Christians will differ on some matters of conscience and culture. One person's liberty, however, must not destroy the faith of a sensitive believer. Conversely, there should not be relational tension over issues of minor importance (Rom. 14–15; 1 Cor. 8–10; Col. 2).

✧ Ecstasy must not be divorced from ethics, and the presence of certain spiritual gifts is not automatically a sign of Christian maturity. Pentecostals must not prize momentary manifestations over the patient acquisition of virtue (1 Cor. 1–4; 13). In fact, the New Testament affirms that spiritual maturity *is* emotional and relational maturity (Peter Scazzero, *The Emotionally Healthy Church*).

✧ Marriage is good, and it carries practical obligations. Singleness requires celibacy, but has its advantages: single women and men have more time and resources for service. The sexual ethics of biblical believers are the most liberating *and* stringent in the world (1 Cor. 6; 2 Cor. 6; Eph. 4; Col. 3; 1 Thess. 4).

✧ Men and women share equally in the grace, fellowship, and callings bestowed by God (Gal. 3:26–29). Husbands and wives need to live in mutual respect, enjoying active, satisfying intimacy and serving their children with loving care (1 Cor. 7; Eph. 5:23—6:4). A healthy marriage is a premier sign of the way Christ loves his church.

✧ God does have appointed spiritual leaders for his church. These include equipping offices (Eph. 4), local and regional church oversight (1 Tim. 3; Titus 1), and evident domains of gifting and service (see Romans 12:6, where the term *charism* is used). These men and women should be held in high regard, and they must validate their calling with holy and humble lives marked by sound doctrine and personal discipline, as well as by enjoying respect both inside and outside of the church.

✧ Prayer and work are equal obligations of true disciples of Jesus Christ (2 Thess. 3; 1 Tim. 2). *The work of the kingdom of God takes place in the world of work, whether at home or in the marketplace.*

✧ Economic and social differences will always exist in the world, but they do not determine fellowship, authority, and vocations in the church community. According to one ancient tradition, the runaway slave Onesimus, featured in Paul's letter to Philemon, would eventually become the bishop of Ephesus! (See Philemon.) The sovereign Spirit calls, anoints, appoints, and distributes gifts according to his pleasure and purpose.

✧ The Lord's Supper creates a radical new sociology as all ages, cultures, and social classes share the bread and cup with sincerity and truth (1 Cor. 10–11). There is no advocacy of violent social revolution—and no place for old divisions and prejudices.

✧ First Peter warns believers that Christian integrity will meet persecution, and James reminds us that all plans for work are subject to the sovereign will of God (James 4:13—5:6). In our enthusiasm for present transformation, eternal perspective must not be lost as we live our lives as "exiles" in this world in reverent fear of the Lord.

PROFILE IN COURAGE[1]

A naval officer aboard a US Navy destroyer served as the crew's unofficial chaplain. During the weekly service and study, all the men (there were no women aboard the ship at this time) were brothers: addressing each other by first names, praying with laughter and tears for their needs, and enjoying worship and discussion focused on the Scriptures. When they departed from the room and went on deck, official protocols were immediately in place and the duties and obligations of rank were in force. This is not dualism, just realism. The differences were profound, as officers swore less and respected their subordinates while the enlisted men went about their work eagerly. The morale improved. A visitor asked the "chaplain" why there was such a positive attitude among so many. The answer: God's grace through the fellowship of the Holy Spirit.

Faith that integrates economics and work propels excellence in all facets of life, even in difficult situations. As you lead your community, challenge believers to offer their best to God 24/7: from how they clean toilets and help demanding customers to rocking colicky babies and confronting narcissistic business partners. Everything changes when believers welcome the Holy Spirit into the "mundane." Suddenly, there is no mundane, as clients are served, work is completed more efficiently, and people are loved and respected for being the image-of-God-bearing, one-of-a-kind works of art that they are (Eph. 2:10).

The Book of Revelation:
Cosmic Battle and Concrete Progress

John Calvin was probably wise not to write a commentary on Revelation, the most controversial and interesting book in the New Testament! The history of interpretation of John's Apocalypse is

---

1 Name withheld by request, due to military sensitivities.

vast and beyond the scope of our discussion here. What is illuminating is the fact that all Christians have found comfort and insight in its pages. One Franciscan scholar summarized the Apocalypse with the question "Who is on the throne?" He then asked that which is the eternal question for every person: "And Who is *your* Sovereign?"

There are three messages for Christians in this panoramic, prophetic work. First, Jesus Christ is Lord, King of kings, the Lamb slain for sinners, and the Lion of Judah arrayed in power and prepared to defeat the enemies of God. Christ is God, Alpha and Omega, the present Sovereign and the coming King. He alone deserves worship and ultimate loyalty, and he will have no competitors for allegiance. There is no room for syncretism (first century: offering of incense to the genius of the emperor-deity; twenty-first century: creation of a personal religion from a smorgasbord of available options). Persecution is expected, and the faithful will be rewarded.

Second, Christ is the head of the Church and calls his people to repentance and renewal. The letters in Revelation 2–3 reveal first-century and every-century challenges for Christian communities: from false teaching to immorality to complacency, from fear to materialism and the danger of renouncing the faith under pressure.

Third, Christians are in a spiritual battle that affects all areas of life. Malevolent economic, religious, and social forces are at work to destroy the church and enslave the global populace. Spiritual warfare is more than confronting obvious cases of demon possession and oppression (though these are real). The battle is ideological, theological, and relational, with adversarial philosophies, heresies, and ethical alternatives arrayed against biblical truth (cf. 1 Cor. 10:1–6; Eph. 6:10–20; Col. 2:6–23).

When discipleship becomes more than a slogan and Christians intentionally bring kingdom principles to work, the fruit is salutary. *But there will be opposition. Integrity in business will confront office politics and the narcissistic and nihilistic proclivities of rivals.* Artistic creativity must confront religious legalism that wants to make all art fit narrow religious categories, while non-Christians attempt to alienate and marginalize the works of serious disciples.

As a leader, you must equip congregants to embrace their work as a calling and a confrontation, as God's work in the world and a battleground for the soul. There is no facile followership. As Dietrich Bonhoeffer said, Christ "bids us to come and die"; and in this cruciform experience we find the resurrection power of the Holy Spirit already at work (Rom. 8).

Living the Future Now:
Applications for New Testament Discipleship

God's reign in Christ is present—and still to come. Every conversion, act of compassion, supernatural manifestation, economic breakthrough, and artistic expression produced by Spirit-empowered believers is a signpost of the future, a foretaste of the eternal kingdom where righteousness (equity/fairness/justice), peace (shalom/concord/healing), and joy (delight in the Lord and his redeeming work) are fully experienced.

We live in the paradox of imperfection as we aspire to holiness (Phil. 3), yet real progress is normal and kingdom influence is measurable. Like yeast (or leaven) in the bread, the mustard seed becoming a great locale for bird nests, and the gospel seed finding good soil in noble hearts, it is possible to see the fruits of God's grace (Matt. 13). We must neither expect perfection nor place artificial limits on the work of God in this age. Somewhere in between coercive theocracy and pessimistic survivalism (waiting in your bunker for the rapture) is the true New Testament teaching to be salt and light (Matt. 5) and to do the work of Jesus while it is day (John 15).

As a leader, your challenge is to create a community ethos of creativity and dependence upon the Spirit. You are called to inquire of the Lord regarding his current purposes for your congregation. You are expected to equip members for daily life, not just for private moments or public religious gatherings. You don't need to be an expert in all domains, but you must help people make connections with other followers of Jesus who are "thinking Christianly" about their fields. In the midst of all the normal sacerdotal tasks, your church must be a safe place to debate, explore, and refine understanding, all in the context of the Great Commandment and Great Commission.

This kind of integrated discipleship is not just a seminar or series of messages—it is the message embedded in all texts and consciously infused into the rhythms of the community. We need more prayer and dialogue so that our message content and ministry structures are serving the mission well.

PROFILE IN COURAGE

Valley Christian Center, Dublin, California

Situated on the top of a hill in a beautiful and prosperous East Bay community, Valley Christian Center is an Assemblies of God church with a multicultural and multidenominational ethos. Senior pastor Roger Valci has been leading a process of spiritual renewal and structural change as the church builds bridges of love and service to the city and valley below.

About two years ago, Pastor Valci began to lead the church in the direction of spiritual renewal, with the baptism in the Spirit and manifestation gifts welcomed in services and all facets of ministry. He made the biblical connection between the empowerment of the Spirit and evangelization. Many believers experienced Spirit-baptism according to Acts 2:4 for the first time, while many practicing Pentecostals among the congregation were renewed and began exercising their gifts.

But this story involves much more than church renewal inside the sanctuary. Pastor Valci connected evangelization with service to the community, particularly involvement in the many nonprofit agencies that serve the elderly, poor, and sick, as well as other mentoring and outreach programs. As of this writing, the members of Valley Christian Center have donated more than sixteen thousand hours of time to more than twenty agencies.

The results are astounding. The mayor and other civic leaders are now friends with the church. Seven other churches have caught the same vision and are mobilizing their members as well. Yes, the church has more visitors and many conversions and baptisms. What is exciting is the connection between spiritual renewal and practical service. Several business leaders are connecting in new ways to foster economic growth and philanthropy.

The baptism of the Spirit is empowerment for service in the kingdom, the promise of Jesus to equip his followers to bring the message of the gospel to all nations. Pastor Valci's church is doing just that—evangelistic moments are numerous, as freshly empowered members find their places of service and look for opportunities at work.

A Command and a Commission

The church has its commission—to reach the world with the gospel. We have the Lord's command that shapes all affections and actions—to love God supremely and our neighbor sacrificially. In the next chapter we will examine more New Testament passages as we look at the practical aspects of fostering economic and social transformation as part of God's redemptive story in and through his people. This is principle four in application: the church creating wealth and demonstrating compassion while carrying out its mission.

Study Questions

1. What sacrifices have we made as followers of Jesus? What have you "given up" in your life of obedience?

2. How can our churches reflect the structures and vitality of Acts and still be relevant for the twenty-first century?

3. Are Spirit-baptism and the manifestation gifts important parts of the public life of your church? If so, why (and how)?

4. What businesses and nonprofit agencies can your church partner with to help your community flourish?

For Further Reading

Ridderbos, Herman N. *The Coming of the Kingdom*. Edited by Raymond O. Zorn. Translated by H. de Jongste. Phillipsburg, NJ: Presbyterian & Reformed, 1962.

Robeck, Cecil M., Jr. *The Azusa Street Mission and Revival: The Birth of the Global Pentecostal Movement*. Nashville: Thomas Nelson, 2006.

Samuel, Vinay, and Chris Sugden, eds. *Mission as Transformation: A Theology of the Whole Gospel*. Oxford: Regnum, 2009.

Scazzero, Peter. *The Emotionally Healthy Church: A Strategy for Discipleship That Actually Changes Lives*. Grand Rapids: Zondervan, 2010.

Valci, Roger. "God's Empowering Presence," "Our Rule of Life," and "The Meeting"—three tracts available at the Valley Christian Center website, www.comediscovervcc.org.

Wright, N. T. *Surprised by Hope: Rethinking Heaven, the Resurrection, and the Mission of the Church*. San Francisco: HarperOne, 2008.

Yong, Amos. *Who Is the Holy Spirit? A Walk with the Apostles*. Brewster, MA: Paraclete, 2011.

The Holy Spirit Empowers Transformation of the Economy and Society

Integrating Faith, Work, and Economics

"Christians have to be twice as smart as they serve God in the world. They not only need to know how to do their jobs well, but they need to know God's perspective on their work."

Os Guinness and John Seel

In AD 249 the Roman emperor Decius unleashed the worst empire-wide persecution of the church in history, demanding that believers offer incense to the genius of the emperor as a god, imprisoning and killing many leaders, confiscating property, and desecrating libraries. By this date, the gospel had permeated all strata of Roman society and the presence of Christian communities stretched from England to India, from Gaul (France) to Ethiopia.

The decree was ferociously enacted in many locales. But in several areas Roman governors were not quite as anxious to be rid of the Christians, even though they shared the emperor's prejudices and owed their appointments to his benevolence. They delayed their implementation because local Christians were the only group of people willing to care for the victims of an awful plague that afflicted many throughout the empire, especially in North Africa.

In the 360s, Emperor Julian tried to turn the empire away from Christianity and back to the old Roman gods and virtues. Called "the apostate" by his foes (he was raised a Christian but rejected the faith as an adult), Julian tried to unleash popular fury against Christians, who, at that time, comprised between 15 and 20 percent of the general population in the urban areas.

His campaign was unsuccessful. One of the emperor's frustrations was that no pagan or non-Christian philosophical community could rival the compassion, generosity, and sacrificial service of the churches.

The gospel transforms each person who believes the message of Jesus' death and resurrection, repents of her or his sin, and embraces Christ as Lord (John 1:11–13; Acts 2:38–39; Rom. 10:9–10). The gospel creates an international community of the Spirit of all who share faith, hope, and love in Jesus Christ (Eph. 3:1–11; 1 Thess. 1).

Care for the broken, poor, and vulnerable, hospitality for the exile and stranger, and the blending of classes and cultures (however imperfectly) is the work of the Holy Spirit. Such sacrificial virtues are only possible when resources are available. These resources occasionally come down from heaven supernaturally (John 6). Most of the time, God's provision comes through hardworking members of the church who offer their time, talent, and treasure as an act of worship.

In this chapter we will explore some key biblical ideas that will propel economic and social transformation. From the revolutionary narrative of Luke to the explosive imperatives of the apostle Paul, there are rich resources for personal, community, and social change that fulfill the eternal purpose of our sovereign Lord and the deepest longings of each human heart.

Romans 12:1–2 as the End of "Religion as Usual"

In the first eleven chapters of his premier epistle, the apostle Paul establishes the reality of human sin (1:18—3:20), the gracious nature of salvation in Christ (1:1–17; 3:21—5:21), the presence of the Holy Spirit to empower true Christian liberty (6:1—8:39), and the inclusion of Gentiles with Jews in the church through faith in Christ (9:1—11:36). These indicatives of grace in chapters 1–11 are united with the imperatives of personal responsibility in chapters 12–15. Paul instructs believers how to live in community (12), love their brothers and sisters as well as outsiders (13), respect each other's differences (14), and carry out the call to evangelize the world (15). This entire section hinges on the first two verses of chapter 12—and these are among the most revolutionary words in Scripture. After eleven chapters on the grace of Christ, Paul presents Christian discipleship as a response to the mercy of God, imperatives that flow from gratitude for grace. Here are Paul's words in various translations for us to consider as we shape our response to the grace of God:

> I appeal to you therefore, brothers, by the mercies of God, to present your bodies as a living sacrifice, holy and acceptable to God, which is your spiritual worship. Do not be conformed to this world, but be transformed by the renewal of your mind, that by testing you may discern what is the will of God, what is good and acceptable and perfect.
>
> Romans 12:1–2 ESV

With eyes wide open to the mercies of God, I beg you, my brothers, as an act of intelligent worship, to give him your bodies, as a living sacrifice, consecrated to him and acceptable by him. Don't let the world around you squeeze you into its own mould, but let God re-mould your minds from within, so that you may prove in practice that the plan of God for you is good, meets all his demands and moves toward the goal of true maturity.

Romans 12:1–2 Phillips

So here's what I want you to do, God helping you: Take your everyday, ordinary life—your sleeping, eating, going-to-work, and walking-around life—and place it before God as an offering. Embracing what God does for you is the best thing you can do for him. Don't become so well-adjusted to your culture that you fit into it without even thinking. Instead, fix your attention on God. You'll be changed from the inside out. Readily recognize what he wants from you, and quickly respond to it. Unlike the culture around you, always dragging you down to its level of immaturity, God brings the best out of you, develops well-formed maturity in you.

Romans 12:1–2 The Message

Romans 12:1–2 forever ends the unbiblical separation of the sacred and secular, the practical and the spiritual sides of life. Sunday worship is no longer radically separate from Monday through Saturday work in the world.

Yes, our community worship experiences are special. Yes, there are seasons of fasting and prayer, times of solitude and service apart from the "daily grind." But the apostle expands the meaning of worship, and our work is part of the offering of our whole selves to God.

Perhaps this doesn't seem radical to some of us. After all, we desire to honor God in all things and be good ambassadors of

Christ, allowing our words and works to glorify God and evoke respect from coworkers and neighbors. But these verses sanctify all facets of life, and they subvert the false dichotomies and hierarchies we create for power or evasion of responsibility. Our private and public life, our play and work, any sacred events or secular engagements, all belong to God.

The Holy Spirit indwells every Christian, and Spirit-baptism is not confined to a special class of leaders. Intimacy with God, integrity with others and self, and impact for Christ in the world is the privilege of each follower of Christ.

Enjoying God and Empowered for Mission

God's creative and redemptive works encompass the whole person, the entire human race, and all of creation (Eph. 1:9–10; Col. 1:15–20). Our Lord Jesus Christ is the firstborn among many brothers and sisters (Rom. 8:29). Paraphrasing C. S. Lewis, Christians do not only believe in the immortality of the soul but in the resurrection of the body. The eternal union with the triune God, the forever life of the redeemed family of God (Rev. 4–5; 7; 20–22), is embodied existence and includes meaningful activity of worship and work.

The Holy Spirit is the "earnest," the "down payment," or the "deposit" of the future. He is the presence and power of God in Christ given to all Christians as a seal/sign of the fullness of salvation that will come with the day of the Lord (2 Cor. 1:21–22; 5:5; Eph. 1:13–14). Jesus promised that his followers would continue his work through the presence of the Holy Spirit (John 7:37–39; 14–16). The reign of God inaugurated in the words and works of Jesus Christ (Matt. 5–9; Luke 4:16–21) continues through his followers. Works of charity, deliverance, healing, forgiveness, peacemaking, reconciliation, and wealth creation are present signposts of the age to come. In other words, *the Holy Spirit empowers the church to live the future now, demonstrating in proclamation and practice what the future looks like when Christ is fully present.* This Spirit-empowered life does not result in perfection in this age, for we see and understand only in part (1 Cor. 13). At the same time, there is no biblical reason to impose artificial limits on the work of God in the world when the conditions of humility, love, unity, and holiness are present (John 17; Eph. 3:14–21).

A Word about Spiritual Gifts

The gifts of the Spirit enable creative integration of faith, work, and wise participation in the economy. It is important to understand the different types of gifts God gives his people. The following is a very compact summation of a large body of literature, decades of pastoral reflection on the work of the Spirit, and a century of Pentecostal consensus and practice.

The Baptism of the Holy Spirit: Acts 2; 8; 10; 19; Romans 8:15–17; 25–27; Ephesians 1:13–14

Pentecostals believe there is a subsequent empowering work of the Holy Spirit that is distinct from regeneration. God anoints his people for mission—giving assurance, boldness, and releasing the gift of tongues for personal edification. All Pentecostals encourage tongues as evidence of this experience, and all agree that God's empowerment needs to be welcomed and received.

Spiritual Expressions and Ministries: What Does Scripture Actually Say? Trinity Life in 1 Corinthians 12

Paul's instructions to the Corinthians unveil a dynamic community experiencing a variety of spiritual expressions and ministries. In today's world of individualism and superspecialization, it is easy to miss the God-honoring and community-building foci of all of God's gifts. In 1 Corinthians 12:1, Paul uses the term *pneumatikon*, introducing the focus of the passage to come. In verses 2 and 3, he reminds his readers that the Holy Spirit will never speak lies about Jesus Christ. Before commenting on the nine *pneumatikoi* (manifestations) in verses 7–11, Paul describes, in verses 4–6, the Trinitarian shape of all Christian activity. The Holy Spirit bestows diverse gifts (*charismaton*/charisms); there are different expressions of service (*diakonion*/the diaconate), but the same Lord [Jesus]; there are a variety of workings (*energematon*/energies or actions), but the same God [the Father] working through all.

All ministry flows from the life of the triune God and is directed toward the glory of God and the good of others. We must resist the temptation to narrow individual vocations too strictly. Conversely, Paul makes it clear at the end of chapter 12 that not all gifts, from apostleship to the interpretation of public speaking in tongues, are given to all believers.

Practically, we can see different facets of service, with some expressions being spontaneous (the nine manifestations of 1 Corinthians 12:8–10) and others having longer duration (the office gifts of apostles, prophets, and teachers in 1 Corinthians 12:28). We must not be divisive or dogmatic, but desire all the gifts to flow in an environment of love and dedication to the purposes of God.

The Manifestations of the Spirit: 1 Corinthians 12–14

The purpose of the "manifestation(s) of the Spirit" in 1 Corinthians 12:7–10 is the edification of the body and the evangelization of unbelievers. These nine expressions are not permanent offices or positions, and they may come to new believers or seasoned veterans. Paul gives some instructions concerning order and proper usage, but he does not reject any gift. It is possible for communities and individuals to mature in discernment and evaluation of these expressions, cognizant that they are imperfect human expressions of the heart and mind of God (1 Cor. 13; 1 Thess. 5:19–21). Sometimes Pentecostals mistake manifestations for spiritual maturity. Other evangelicals and Roman Catholics often look at enthusiasm and spontaneity as signs of immaturity. Biblical teaching corrects both errors. God desires to strengthen his people and bestow resources for mission.

Here is an important insight: In 1 Corinthians 12–14, Paul is correcting some practices and encouraging vitality in church gatherings. There is no indication, however, that these or any other expressions of the life of Spirit are confined to church gatherings. One of the defining marks of gospel life is "signs and wonders" that accompany evangelization. A flourishing believer will be open to supernatural wisdom and understanding as he or she carries out daily labors, removing all false separations between "spiritual" and "secular" and leading toward integration that brings glory to God and allows even unbelievers to glorify God for the good works they observe in Christians (Matt. 5:16).

PROFILE IN COURAGE

A Personal Testimony

Over thirty years ago, I was invited to give a lecture on "Divine Omniscience and Human Free Will" in a secular community college philosophy class. The professor was a well-known atheist, hostile to religion and happy to undermine the simple faith of college freshmen. He told the class, "If God knows the future, then none of our decisions are truly free. Therefore, either God is ignorant or we are mere robots." The challenge was set: Would I be his next victim or present something that silences his appeals to emotion and flawed logic?

I studied well and presented a classic Christian case (from Scripture, Augustine, and other philosophers) for both divine sovereignty and human free will. The class was quiet and respectful, and even the professor only interrupted once for clarification. As I concluded I suddenly called out to a student in the back of the room: "Bernie, when this class is done, you will walk across the quad, go into the cafeteria, get a Coke from the machine, and sit at a corner table with your friends. Am I correct?"

The student was in shock. "How did you know my name and what I do every time this class is over?"

I replied, "The same way God knows all things and you are free to carry on your life."

Here is the surprise: I had no natural knowledge of the student's name or his habits after class. The Holy Spirit bestowed knowledge in the moment, and my lecture now had impact.

And here is the rest of the story. One of the students in that class came to Christ a few weeks later and went on to significant ministry. A couple of others came to faith in the ensuing months, with the seeds sown in this class providing the impetus for exploring the claims of Christ. Praise God for his sovereign grace!

By the way, not all my lectures have manifestations of the Spirit. If we are open to the Lord, however, the gifts can flow in unexpected ways—even outside the church.

PROFILE IN COURAGE

Whitefield and Wesley

George Whitefield was an eloquent Anglican minister, a partner with John and Charles Wesley in the evangelical awakening of the mid-eighteenth century. Whitefield was the first great outdoor evangelist, speaking to thousands in open fields and seeing extraordinary experiences of awakening, conversion, and transformation in his hearers. Knowing that he needed partners in both preaching and organization, he asked his friends to join him.

As a highly disciplined and proper man, John Wesley was

reluctant to take his ministry outside the church walls. Fortunately for the future of evangelical Christianity, he overcame his reticence and traveled for more than fifty years in successful work. He discovered that God's power and presence was not confined to ecclesial locales.

Whitefield and Wesley often disagreed theologically; Whitefield humbly confessed, however, that without Wesley's discipleship structures his meetings and oratory would have been "a rope of sand."

Daily life is charged with possibilities when we begin to view things from God's perspective.

The Charisms of Romans 12

Western Christians love systematic categories. The variety of testing instruments designed to help Christians discover their gifts reveals a penchant for self-knowledge. The Holy Spirit, however, is not bound to our constructs, and humility is the order of the day when it comes to understanding how God is working. In Romans 12:3–8, Paul encourages believers to exercise their gifts (*charisms*) in a context of confidence *and* humility, seeking to build up the body. The seven expressions/functions listed seem to be general areas of service that arose in the course of the Holy Spirit's development of the church. It is interesting that prophecy is in the same list as serving and that leadership gifts function with mercy and encouraging. These charisms are essential for effective work; and when the local church is an incubator of transformation for the community, they find new expression "outside the walls."

Local and Regional Church Leaders:
Acts 6; 20; 1 Timothy 3; Titus 1

Episcopal (bishop-centric), presbyterian (local/regional councils), and congregational (local church autonomy) forms of church governance all find their foundations in New Testament texts and the experiences of the early church. Pentecostal movements employ all of these forms, with some groups acknowledging bishops (as well as functioning apostles and prophets) and others stressing the wisdom of elderships locally and regionally. All traditions affirm that local churches need spiritual oversight (elders/pastors/shepherds/priests) and practical service (deacons/deaconesses/vestries). These offices are gifts from God and affirmed by the witness of the Spirit in the community.

Equipping Ministries: Ephesians 4

The risen Christ has appointed apostles, prophets, evangelists, and pastoral/teaching gifts for the equipping and maturation of every member of the body of Christ (Eph. 4:11–13). The corpus of literature (and some amount of controversy) on these offices is vast. Pentecostals generally affirm that all these functions are in operation, with apostles, prophets, and evangelists exercising translocal leadership and influence while the pastors and teachers focus on local empowerment. The important thing is that those who have these gifts not only "do the work" but also multiply the same work in others and contribute experientially to the unity Paul proclaims in Ephesians 4:1–16. This unity is the answer to the prayer of the Lord Jesus Christ in John 17, particularly verses 20–21.

The focus of discipleship must be on all of God's people walking in their callings and expressing those vocations in the world of work and active participation in economic and social flourishing—from the general charisms of Romans 12 to the appointed offices of Ephesians 4 and 1 Timothy 3—while being open to releasing manifestations according to the leading of the Spirit. Rather than being confined to church buildings, it is vital that all these gifts are integrated into all the domains of kingdom work. Here are some thoughts taken from the Bible and historical reflection on its application:

The Goodness of Work

In both Scripture and church history, the church has wrestled with how to reconcile the lively hope of the imminent return of Jesus Christ with the practical realities of everyday living. Remember, work is not a curse and labor is not a result of the fall. Sin has perverted legitimate work into fruitless toil. The words of the Teacher inflame the conscience: "I saw that all labor and all achievement spring from man's envy of his neighbor. This too is meaningless, a chasing after the wind" (Eccl. 4:4). One writer's observations of human futility must not frame a full theology of work. Beginning with Abraham, continuing with the community life of Israel, and culminating in the incendiary community of the church, God clearly unveils the goodness of work. From the Spirit-empowered craftsmanship of the tabernacle (Ex. 25; 35) to the practical management of property and economic fairness (Lev. 25; Neh. 5; Amos 2; 5), honest labor, stewardship of personal property, and social concern have been part of the worldview of God's people.

Biblical Insights Regarding Discipleship and Work

The new believers in Thessalonica faced a variety of voices, with some speakers offering "revelations" that the day of the Lord had already come and gone and some hyperreligious people, who were too spiritual to work, living off the largesse of the community. Ever the wise pastor and theologian, Paul lays out a balanced framework that keeps hope alive and grounds ethical behavior.

He assures his Thessalonian friends that the day of the Lord is still in the future (they have not missed out on it) and that this hope will give them strength in the midst of persecution (1 Thess. 4–5; 2 Thess. 1–2). Paul also encourages spiritual growth in faith, hope, and love, calling for holy living free from ungodly passions and for positive relationships in the community (1 Thess. 1; 4–5; 2 Thess. 3). In the midst of what seems to be a standard call to spiritual vitality (including spiritual gifts—1 Thess. 5:19–21), Paul inserts his most practical teaching of all:

> In the name of the Lord Jesus Christ, we command you, brothers, to keep away from every brother who is idle and does not live according to the teaching you received from us. For you yourselves know how you ought to follow our example. We were not idle when we were with you, nor did we eat anyone's food without paying for it. On the contrary, we worked night and day, laboring and toiling so that we would not be a burden to any of you. We did this, not because we do not have the right to such help [for preaching the gospel and shepherding the new flock], but in order to make ourselves a model for you to follow. For even when we were with you, we gave you this rule: "If a man will not work, he shall not eat."
>
> We hear that some among you are idle. They are not busy; they are busybodies. Such people we command and urge in the Lord Jesus Christ to settle down and earn the bread they eat. And as for you, brothers, never tire of doing what is right.

2 Thessalonians 3:6–13

Key insights for twenty-first-century discipleship are embedded in this passage. Before expounding on the positive aspects of Paul's encouragement to these new Christians, let's see what is *not* being said:

✧ Paul is not invalidating financial support for ministry vocations. That would contradict his teachings elsewhere (1 Cor. 9:1–18; Gal. 6:6).

⟡ Paul is not repudiating helping the disabled and the poor (see Acts 11:27–30 and Paul's words in 2 Corinthians 8–9 concerning the offering for the distressed Christians in Jerusalem). He is not offering a systemic policy on the role of the church or public agencies in regard to poverty.

⟡ Paul is not advocating "burnout for Jesus" or extreme work hours. "Night and day" refers to the season of sacrificial service and the tireless efforts of apostolic mission.

Paul is affirming key principles that establish practical foundations for the Christian's work in the world:

⟡ We are made to work. To paraphrase Dorothy Sayers, author of the delightful work *Are Women Human?* we are human beings created by God with a job to do; we do our jobs as men or women.

⟡ The nearness of the Lord's return is not a reason to quit our everyday work. In fact, Christ expects us to be at our assigned "posts" and faithful in our God-given assignments when he returns (Matt. 24–25).

⟡ "Ministry" may be funded by donations; however, those who are "working priests"—a term that actually describes all believers (1 Peter 2:4–10), as well as current notions of bivocational parish leaders—are not less spiritual than those paid from the tithes and offerings of God's people.

If all of life is an offering to God and labor is good, then current disconnects between church and work are contrary to the will of God. Pentecostal Christians are no more or no less guilty than other traditions when it comes to separating spiritual and practical, church and work, sacred and secular domains. From the Azusa Street Revival to today's summer camps, Pentecostals exalt the "call to full-time ministry" and unwittingly create a hierarchy of clerical and lay leadership that consciously and unconsciously disempowers and disenfranchises many of God's people.

PROFILE IN COURAGE

Brett and Lyn Johnson, The Ministry of Business:
The Story of The Institute and rēp
(www.inst.net and www.repurposing.biz)

Brett and Lyn Johnson have led consultations with about three hundred companies and organizations and equipped over eighty-four hundred business missionaries. They have a number of interconnected products under The Institute for Innovation, Integration & Impact (called The Institute), with the purpose of "Repurposing leaders and corporations to discover and implement personal and corporate callings, thereby transforming communities and nations." They used to operate part of what they do as a nonprofit, but since 2007 have integrated everything under the umbrella of The Institute with the combined tagline of "Repurposing Business—Transforming Society®." The Johnsons' list of corporate, nonprofit, and governmental clients is impressive. What is most impressive, though, is the integration that is the heart of all they do. They have products such as Repurposing Business®, LEMON Leadership®, Transforming Society®, and Convergence that address the needs of various constituents.

Brett and Lyn are deeply committed to transformation of all the domains/spheres of kingdom life. In the early 1980s they were suddenly thrust into local church leadership as elders of a church confronted with the moral failure of the pastor. When they moved to the United States five years later they left a healthy church that had planted other churches, all without hiring a full-time cleric. A passion for the apostolic calling of the laity (to paraphrase Pope John Paul II) was born and continues to burn brightly.

Descriptions of the Johnsons' publications unveil profound insight into the opportunities for global engagement:

Convergence: ending compartmentalization and liberating each person to grasp and fulfill her/his life purpose.

LEMON Leadership: helping *L*uminaries, *E*ntrepreneurs, *M*anagers, *O*rganizers, and *N*etworkers discover how they are wired, develop their callings consistent with their identities, sharpen their skills, and improve in other arenas in order to maximize impact.

Repurposing Capital: exactly what the title implies—a kingdom look at faith-based financing, money, investment, and a return to biblical economics.

Transforming Society: it is not enough to experience personal fulfillment; the kingdom of God embraces the city, the nation, and all facets of life.

The Ministry of Business: Abraham was a businessman on a mission—called by God to bless the nations; today's business leaders can discover and complete their God-given mission.

Beyond Halfway: insights for church leaders on how to equip businesspeople in their congregations for whole-life discipleship.

Brett and Lyn train well-educated and experienced professionals in kingdom principles and form missional teams to consult around the world. Their clients are found in China, Egypt, India, Indonesia, Israel, Nigeria, South Africa, the United States, and other nations. Brett and Lyn are intentional about integrating the leading of the Spirit, best practices, and biblical principles. They have seen amazing results from their consultations, even with clients who were not fully committed to Christ—from physical healing and miracles to reconciled marriages to opportunities to help different governments frame monetary policy.

For decades Brett has encouraged clients and leaders to stop pursuing the ever-elusive goal of "balance" and aim for true integration. How we frame our goals matters, and the world will be better off with fewer works of "three steps to . . ." or "achieving balance" and more focus on connecting faith with all facets of life, especially the work that occupies most of our waking hours.

Please note that the call to ministry is not in question. There are many biblical and historical examples of ministry vocation (Ex. 3–6; Isa. 6; Jer. 1; John 1:19–34; Acts 9; Rom. 15:15–16), and the sacerdotal responsibilities of those anointed by the Spirit and affirmed by the church are vital for its health. God does call leaders, and Christ has established delegated authority. Regardless of ecclesiastical tradition, appointed offices are part of the plan of God for the equipping and maturing of believers (Eph. 4:1–16; 1 Tim. 3; Titus 1).

The problem arises from a weak theology of discipleship and work and the self-interest that creeps into ecclesial structures. From the fearful Israelites compromising their holy calling (Ex. 18–19, especially 19:6) to two millennia of church members leaving the "spiritual stuff" to the ministers and priests, both clergy and laity have compromised their vocations. The call for spiritual leaders to equip and empower all of God's people is muffled by the unbiblical class structure and self-serving systems of religious professionals. The laity too often accepted this state of affairs, with the results of abject submission or barely concealed contempt (especially among business professionals who fund the operations).

Toward Integration

The solution is not anarchistic destruction of ecclesial structures and homogenization of Christian work. A robust theology of the priesthood of all believers joined with the full gospel of reconciliation (2 Cor. 5:14—6:2) will transform individuals, communities, and ecclesial structures while honoring proper authority and sacerdotal vocations.

A Note about Money

Another tragic consequence of the false secular/spiritual division is the confusion about money that reigns in the church. Cynics in both business and the church often say, "Vision is spelled M-O-N-E-Y." The courting and favoring of the well-to-do by those in "spiritual" work is evident, while many called to ministry glorify poverty and "living by faith." While not judging the unique path of any follower of Jesus, this confusion needs to be corrected. Local church leaders are urging their congregants to tithe and get out of personal debt, while Christian colleges and universities place thousands of students in five- and six-figure bondage. Do we see the contradiction? Audiences are called to surrender all for the mission, while many of the leaders proclaiming such sacrifice already have their "mansions."

God does call some to voluntary poverty. God also calls some to risk-and-reward efforts that create jobs and transform economies. A Pentecostal venture capitalist said to me in 2001, "You preach and a thousand folks are blessed. That is important. But remember, I make a decision and a thousand people gain or lose employment. Which one is the greater work?"

Empowered for Compassion and Economic Growth: Insights for the Local Church

How do we begin to make application for our local churches? In the next chapter, we will take a look at three practical facets of discipleship that will unleash clarity and productivity among church members. In chapter 6, we will offer a vision of the local church as an "incubator" of "sociomissional transformation" (translation: every believer empowered and equipped for full impact in society). At this point in our journey, we need to catch our breath and consider some economic wisdom that comes from our reflection on biblical truth and Christian history.

For two millennia, believers have been part of local and global economies. Like most of humankind, Christians have labored for their daily bread: working in fields and factories, as artisans and executives, as homemakers and service personnel. Christians have been at the forefront of global economic and social progress, either as leaders of or as participants in new movements that increase human flourishing.

PROFILE IN COURAGE

The Protestant Work Ethic and the Challenge of Prosperity

The Protestant Reformation of the sixteenth century highlighted the priesthood of all believers and the dignity of all vocations. Spiritual leaders were respected, but the laity was honored and their labors celebrated as part of God's plan for the world. In addition to preparing for heaven, a Christian's calling includes the fruit of his or her labor as part of the civilizing task of creation and the redeeming work of Christ as God's kingdom becomes ever more fully present.

As a result of this expanded worldview, work was no longer merely an offering to priests and princes and a means of survival until death and passage to the afterlife. Creative, ethical, and innovative "secular" work glorifies God and contributes to the progress of the kingdom. The economic progress unleashed by this fresh understanding of biblical truth was (and is) immeasurable.

Even with this good theology and a sense of divine blessing upon prosperity, the gap between the sacred and secular remained wide. Economics and work were still seen as instrumental for mission rather than the mission itself.

At the dawn of the twentieth century, global Pentecostal Christianity burst upon the scene, with empowered believers urgent to complete the Great Commission in light of the imminent return of Jesus Christ. This urgency was so strong that in the early days of the Azusa Street Revival in Los Angeles (1906–09) William Seymour told his friends to forego planting new churches and "get people saved, sanctified, and filled with the Holy Ghost" so that they could lead as many as possible to Jesus in the short time left.

From the multicultural revival of Azusa, to the Bible Women in India and the Methodists in Chile, Pentecostals sought the revitalization of the church and the evangelization of the world in the power of the Spirit. As they were thrust into the harvest fields, they "accidently" found themselves creating orphanages, medical clinics, feeding programs, small businesses, Bible training schools, and a host of other agencies and projects as part of the mission.

The growing edge of the global church is overwhelmingly Pentecostal/charismatic, with the vast majority of non-Western Christians embracing some form of Spirit-baptism, the validity of spiritual gifts, and the realities of spiritual warfare and supernatural experiences. But Pentecostals of all kinds are now maturing in their understanding of God's kingdom and discovering the responsibilities that come with being Christ's ambassadors to their societies.

Economic Maxims

A survey of Scripture and reflection on economic and ecclesial history produces some maxims of economic wisdom that can help guide our discernment as we commission the people of God to their daily tasks. The following is a starting point as local churches take responsibility for economic and social change:

- ✦ A free market must be rooted in virtue and the rule of law. From the thirteenth to the early twentieth century, economics was a subdiscipline of moral philosophy.

- ✦ The Bible has much to say about economics and work, including insights on debt, giving, saving, the challenge of greed and blessings of hard work, community care, and personal industriousness.

- ✦ "Life stewardship" is one way of framing our daily tasks as we fulfill our vocations. This includes personal, family, church, and social management of God's resources, relationships, and opportunities.

✧ We need to help people understand how the economy works locally and globally so that they are not mere dependents/victims or exploiters, but contributors to the greater good.

✧ Economics is a driver for cultural entrepreneurship and innovation.

✧ A Christian way will be loved and hated—loved for its prosperous outcomes and hated for the values that built these outcomes.

✧ Local churches are "base camps" for launching "cultural entrepreneurs" who are connective tissue between faith and economics, charity and outreach, evangelization and improvement of the world.

✧ People and companies succeed by creating value for others, not by extracting value from others.

✧ Individuals, communities, towns, states, and nations must produce more than they consume, earn more than they spend.

✧ Only value-creating work leads to long-term economic growth, and long-term growth reduces poverty and helps people flourish.

✧ We have a stewardship responsibility to pass on a thriving economy to future generations.

✧ Economic dependency and spiritual dependency are mutually reinforcing—the opposite is empowerment.

✧ Redistribution of wealth for its own sake does not create economic justice.

❖ "Prosperity" varies according to ability, culture, location, opportunity, and spiritual climate; however, all believers, churches, and communities can create value and wealth, improve living standards, and achieve measurable progress without moral compromise.

The aim of our integration of faith, work, and economics is not conservatism or liberalism. The aim is the glory of God and the flourishing of our communities. As mentioned earlier, Jesus does not fit into tidy ideological or political boxes. Compassion and generosity are givens. As Robert A. Sirico has commented, to meet the poor is a Christological event. Jesus often comes to us in the "distressing disguise" (Mother Teresa and Michael Card) of the needy. If we can help someone in need, Christian love compels action.

Flourishing is more than charity. It is fulfilling God-given callings as individuals, local churches, and larger networks of relationship and vocation. It is God's will that the life of the future become present in all arenas. So what prevents us from flourishing? The short answer is sin. Whether it is personal peccadilloes or social structures, sin permeates our existence and inhibits our flourishing.

Thanks to the work of Christ, we have provision for forgiveness, redemption, and transformation so that we are no longer slaves to sin. But this great salvation is a process, involving the work of the Spirit leading us to personal wholeness, relational integrity, and vocational clarity. It is to these facets of discipleship that we now turn.

Study Questions

1. What examples of Christians at work do you admire?
2. How do you contribute to the flourishing of your community?
3. How should the church engage in helping the poor? What are the proper roles of local, state, and national governments in alleviating poverty?

4. In your context, what does it mean to be "rich" or "middle-class" or "poor"?

For Further Reading

Claar, Victor V., and Robin J. Klay. *Economics in Christian Perspective: Theory, Policy, and Life Choices.* Downers Grove, IL: InterVarsity, 2007.

Foster, Richard J. *The Challenge of the Disciplined Life: Christian Reflections on Money, Sex, and Power.* New York: HarperCollins, 1985.

Johnson, Brett. *Repurposing Capital.* Saratoga, CA: Indaba Publishing, 2010.

Robison, James, and Jay W. Richards. *Indivisible: Restoring Faith, Family, and Liberty Before It Is Too Late.* New York: FaithWords, 2012.

Ideal Meets Real | 5

Personal Wholeness, Relational Integrity, and Vocational Clarity

G. K. Chesterton once quipped to the critics of Christianity that the faith has not been tried and found wanting—it has been found difficult and rarely tried. The Bible is full of the gracious activity of God as he delivers, forgives, heals, and restores. In Christ, full provision is made for our justification (no "rap sheet" in heaven—Colossians 2:13–14) and our sanctification (the Holy Spirit empowering the new life in us—Romans 8). John seems severe in his first epistle when he makes obedience to Christ's commands the proof of authentic conversion. But in the next breath this sensitive shepherd tells us that all the commands are focused in the Great Command to love one another (1 John 2–4).

Christian discipleship is nothing less than conformity to Christ—as individual believers and as local communities. The very life of God is in us. The Bible says it so many ways: "Christ in you, the hope of glory" (Col. 1:27). "It is God who works in you to will and to act according to his good purpose" (Phil. 2:13). Jesus is declared to be the firstborn among brothers and unafraid to call all believers his siblings (Rom. 8:28–30; Heb. 2:11).

The content of Christian discipleship is found in the Great Commandment of Matthew 22:37–40. All the Law and the Prophets, Jesus said, are summed up in the command to love God with all your heart, soul, and mind, and to love your neighbor as yourself. It takes a lifetime of cooperation with the Spirit of God and participation with the people of God to live out these words. The image below places these expectations in visual array and reminds us that all of these "loves" grow together:

God's Life—Growing in Us!

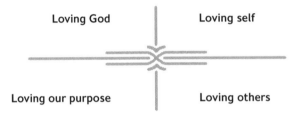

Loving God	Loving self
Loving our purpose	Loving others

At the center is the triune God: our Father, the Almighty, who is also Abba; our Lord Jesus Christ, King of Kings, Bridegroom, and Brother; and the Holy Spirit, the creative power of the cosmos and the very presence of God in us. As we look at the visual, we see the interconnected facets of our life in Christ.

God's Invitation

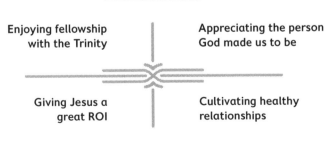

Enjoying fellowship with the Trinity	Appreciating the person God made us to be
Giving Jesus a great ROI	Cultivating healthy relationships

We have a divine invitation to intimacy with God. This will transform our inner life and engender integrity and proper love of self, healing the hurts and delivering us from our addiction to self. Healthy, intentional relationships are possible as we grow in Christ and proper self-worth. If we are in step with the Spirit, we will discern our particular life purpose and begin fulfilling it well. This quadrant works for congregations as well as individuals, as leaders help the community experience the presence of God, align with God's mission, cultivate friendships inside and outside, and complete their part of the Great Commission.

Here is another way of visualizing the tapestry God is weaving within each person and local church:

Biblical Application

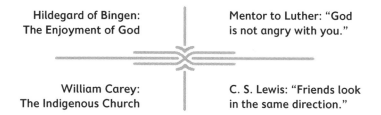

Hildegard of Bingen:
The Enjoyment of God

Mentor to Luther: "God is not angry with you."

William Carey:
The Indigenous Church

C. S. Lewis: "Friends look in the same direction."

A Transformational Quartet

Discipleship is nothing less than transformation as believers, churches, and the body of Christ—transformation in which we receive "grace upon grace" (John 1:16 ESV), experience a life of "faith to faith" (Rom. 1:17 KJV), and move from "glory to glory" through the work of the Spirit of God (2 Cor. 3:17–18 KJV). In practical terms, the integration of faith, work, and economics in the context of the Great Commission and in obedience to the Great Commandment means that we are called to:

Spiritual Formation (the underpainting on the canvas). We cultivate intimacy with God through the spiritual disciplines and awakening to the inner work of the Spirit. This is the "Loving God" part of the image above. Though this is intensely personal, it does not take place in isolation. We need community to grow as we pray and play, worship and work, for the Lord.

Personal Wholeness. Our whole being is being healed and transformed as we become psychologically and spiritually healthy. This corresponds to "Loving Self" in the quadrant above. Here we see the character and nature of God changing us from the inside out (2 Peter 1:1–9).

Relational Integrity. With God's help we can move from oppression and repression, codependency and dysfunction, to healthy liberty that can love and laugh, set good boundaries, and understand the relational dynamics of our life situations. Relational integrity is foundational for employers and employees and for all economic and social interactions. This is "Loving Others" joyfully.

Vocational Clarity. Understanding our personality, strengths, spiritual gifts, and specific life purpose does not guarantee a lifetime of perfect jobs, but it will help guide us to the right field of work and shape *how* we work. When the universal calling of stewardship is united with specific understanding of our part in God's plan, there is great fulfillment. We can know and love "Our Purpose."

Growth in these areas of discipleship does not happen in a circumstantial vacuum. Most people cannot take a few years off from family, school, or work just to do "spiritual stuff." God's design for our lives unfolds in the realities of daily life as the ways of God are applied to particular facets of our life.

Whole Life Discipleship

Personal Wholeness and Our Work

As the Holy Spirit matures, sanctifies, and transforms each believer into the image of Christ (Rom. 6:11–14; 8:28–30; 2 Cor. 3:17–18), powerful redemptive work is taking place in our inner being—and even in our bodies, as our hearts and habits change. Healthy people are healthy workers, whether their activities take place inside or outside of the church. This book is focused on faith, work, and economics, so the implications of personal wholeness will be centered on its impact on work and participation in economic and social transformation.

Gospel wholeness begins with believers understanding all that happens when they receive Christ as Lord (John 1:12–13). God's grace in Christ is amazing. Through no merit of our own and by the power of the Spirit, we are blessed to be called by each of the following:

Justified: By the sacrifice of Christ, we can stand before God clothed in Christ's righteousness, free from accusation and enjoying full access to God's favor and presence (Rom. 3:21–31; 5:1–11).

Regenerated ("born again"—John 3:3–8): We are not only free from accusation—God the Holy Spirit lives in us and makes us alive and able to walk in the ways of God. We are not merely "improved"; we have a brand-new nature.

Sanctified: We can progressively say no to sin and yes to loving obedience as we surrender our will to God's will and allow the Spirit to lead us (Rom. 6; 8). Yes, we still stumble, but we can overcome the habits, hang-ups, and hurts of our history.

Adopted: As sons and daughters of the Father and co-heirs with our Lord Jesus Christ, we have a new identity as part of the new humanity redeemed by the blood of the Lamb (Rom. 8; Gal. 3:26—4:7; Rev. 4–5; 12). Even if our natural upbringing was abusive and broken, redemption and restoration has begun and our future is no longer tethered to our past.

Raised and seated with Christ: We do not serve God in order to ascend a ladder and hope for heaven someday. We serve as royal priests secure in our favored position and voluntarily humbling ourselves, living as servants of all (Mark 10:42–45; Phil. 2:5–11).

"Saved": This is often the overarching term used for all the others, but in this context it speaks of deliverance and liberation from sin and adversarial spiritual powers that threaten our fruitfulness (2 Cor. 10:1–6; Eph. 6:10–20; Col. 2:11–15). We are free from ideological, philosophical, and spiritual traps that undermine God's work in and through us.

Question: "Wonderful theology, Professor. What does it have to do with the economy and work?"

Answer: "Everything!"

All six facets of God's grace are at work in believers, but transformation takes time. As God is working in us (Phil. 2:12–13), consider the following contributions that becoming-more-like-Christ people can make.

First, *healthy people create healthy workplaces in the home, in ministry, in the factories and the fields, in break rooms and boardrooms.* Secure people are less likely to abuse those they lead or subvert those above them. Believers learning to overcome sin and to be alert to spiritual dynamics will avoid the moral and political pitfalls awaiting them and positively contribute to a fairer, more enjoyable workplace.

Second, *whole people help others to become whole and to see life in light of a new identity in Christ instead of the victimhood of past prejudices and traumas.* These are not pie-in-the-sky piety and platitudes, but intentional, robust efforts to influence growth in others.

Third, *work finds its proper place in the lives of those who are experiencing personal wholeness.* Work is no longer either all-consuming or marginal. Work and participation in the larger economy are positioned within the Great Commission and Great Commandment and become part of "living the future now" as disciples faithfully fulfill their callings.

Relational Integrity and Transformation of the Economy

The economy—local and global—is built on confidence and trust, undergirded by the rule of law and virtue. From the thirteenth to the nineteenth century, serious economists framed their work as a branch of moral philosophy and recognized that free trade, exchange of value, and all facets of business depended upon moral people considering the good of others as well as their own.

All of life is relational. From our walk with God to daily work, we are part of an amazing web of relationships. An isolated introvert working on a computer still depends on other people who keep the Internet humming. Our impact for Christ depends on healthy and prudent interaction with others.

Three implications for integrated discipleship are rooted in relational integrity. The first is honest communication and covenant-keeping. Playing by the rules and telling the truth (by that I don't mean unwise sharing of emotions or untimely communication) are vital for any workplace and for confidence that will propel economic investments. Integrity means we mean what we say and say what we mean. Integrity means we adhere to our agreements and offer excellence in our efforts.

Second, relational integrity opens new avenues for collaboration and partnership, thus helping churches and communities to flourish and fulfill God's plan for the world. Imagine two congregations in a community trusting each other and synergizing their efforts to create jobs, help the local schools, and offer care to the hurting—all in the name of Jesus and with a clear call to faith shared at the proper time. Competition yields to cooperation as the dominant disposition that drives new initiatives, and abundance replaces scarcity.

Third, relational integrity retains clients and customers and creates prosperity beyond the bottom line of one organization. Integrity can "go viral" as its fruits are "caught" by others. As spiritual leaders instruct and inspire congregants, they can challenge employers to create better conditions and employees who excel in all their tasks. A culture of confidence and trust will begin to overcome corruption and covetousness.

Vocational Clarity and Twenty-First-Century Work

Vocational clarity occurs when believers understand that their new identity in Christ aligns with God's revealed will in Scripture and they begin to grasp their specific role in the body of Christ and broader society. Clarity includes knowledge of natural strengths and spiritual gifts, specific callings, and skills that add value in chosen fields of work.

Flourishing churches and communities depend upon all parts of the body fulfilling their functions. God's callings and gifts are not static—they are dynamic as Christians learn to live by the Spirit and keep in step with the Spirit (Rom. 8:1–17; Gal. 5:22–26). Vocational clarity is not overspecialization or vague feelings but rather increasing wisdom regarding the value each person brings to the mission or the task.

Vocational clarity will enhance flexibility and make maturing believers more employable in an ever-changing labor market. Regardless of college major or past positions in industry, Christians who are clear about their abilities and value will have greater opportunities. Such flexibility is not just for the highly educated or technologically skilled; it is the privilege of every child of the King. There are no inferior or superior people, just unique assignments.

Spiritual leaders must also bring reality into the conversation. To say that anyone can do anything they imagine is a lie. Visualizing possibilities can either be the first step in God's plan or a fantasy that keeps us from God's best for our lives. Imagining a career in opera without a good singing voice is fruitless. Conversely, ability without discipline is equally wrongheaded.

Clarity begins in the presence of God—with humility and joy, repentance and faith. Clarity is fostered as we obey the general precepts of God's Word. One Scottish preacher declared to a group of young leaders, "You will have many more crises of obedience than guidance. Obey what is clear in the Bible and you will position yourself to hear from God about your specific assignments."

The Big Picture in Review

God has a plan to glorify himself and share his triune life with redeemed humanity. His plan unfolds in history, through people who spend much of their time working and contributing to the economy. God's transforming work in the world takes place through the local and global church. Discipleship must include the economy and daily work without being consumed by materialism or ideology. Life in the Spirit means that what we do today is a signpost of the kingdom of God that is already here in part and will be revealed in fullness when Christ returns in glory. Personal wholeness, relational integrity, and vocational clarity in each believer and in every church community will unleash a tidal wave of creativity and productivity.

How does all this take place? In and through the local church. People in a place with a purpose are the resource God is using to redeem the world. The local church can become the catalyst for spiritual and social transformation.

Study Questions

1. What discipleship-related classes and programs are in place in your church? How do they address the world of work?

2. What formal and/or informal mentors have helped you discover more about yourself—e.g., helped bring you greater vocational clarity?

3. What value do you bring to your workplace, beyond fulfilling your specific daily tasks?

4. How can our churches help the unemployed and underemployed?

For Further Reading

Jarrett, Bryan. *Extravagant: Living Out Your Response to God's Outrageous Love.* Springfield, MO: Influence Resources, 2011.

McGinnis, Alan Loy. *The Friendship Factor: How to Get Closer to the People You Care For.* Philadelphia: Augsburg Fortress, 2004.

Mostert, Johan and Charlie Self, *Discipleship Dynamics(TM),* http://www.discipleshipdynamics.com/

Scazzero, Peter. *The Emotionally Healthy Church: A Strategy for Discipleship That Actually Changes Lives.* Grand Rapids: Zondervan, 2010.

Tozer, A. W. *The Knowledge of the Holy: The Attributes of God: Their Meaning in the Christian Life.* New York: HarperCollins, 1978.

The Local Church | 6

Incubator of Transformation

As we reflect on this material, it is vital to remember that the local church is still the primary community through which God's people worship, grow, evangelize, and demonstrate compassion—even though the church-as-organization is not called to do every task in God's world. The major idea in this primer is that all spheres of life are ordained by God and can be infused with the Holy Spirit's wisdom.

Every believer and spiritual leader is a part of the body of Christ in at least four ways. First, a Christian's connection with a local, tangible community is assumed in the New Testament. Whether the parish is large or small, with or without a permanent building, cell-group focused or celebrating in a huge stadium, personal purpose is not fulfilled without others. Second, most churches are part of formal or informal denominations, movements, networks, or traditions that foster accountability, relationships, resource-sharing, and missional cooperation. The third area of participation is the sense of place. Believers are part of the church that functions in a specific city, region, and nation, with particular cultural and linguistic characteristics that are on-the-ground realities of the mission. It is important that Christians and their congregations reach out to the communities next door in order to bring the full presence of the kingdom to their geographical locale. Finally, followers of Jesus are part of the global body of Christ and the historic communion of the saints (Heb. 12:1–3). Solidarity with the suffering church (Heb. 10:32–39; Rev. 4–5), strategic alliances for civilizational and missional progress, and joyous delight in the unity-in-diversity of Trinitarian believers enhances personal and community vitality.

Integrated thinking will not diffuse or weaken "church work." If more congregants volunteer in local nonprofits, engage in new business ventures, and see their work as worship, some clergy will fear a loss of volunteers for their programs. What integration does is compel discernment, prayer, and strategic thinking among leaders and members. New questions emerge if the biblical goals enumerated in this book are central to God's purposes. Instead of asking how many folks can help with a program or what "real commitment" means in terms of attendance, kingdom-centric leaders are asking different types of questions:

✧ How are all the activities of our church contributing to discipleship for people of all ages and stages of the Christian life?

✧ Are we communicating discipleship outcomes that people understand and connect with their spiritual disciplines?

✧ Are we fostering excitement and educational environments that enable humble believers to hear God's call and find resources to become influencers in their domains?

✧ Are we wise in how we speak of work, ennobling all aspects of daily life: from parenthood to customer service, from leadership to productivity, from volunteer efforts to civic leadership?

✧ Are we welcoming the work of the Holy Spirit in our public worship, study classes, and small groups—learning and maturing in our exercise of the manifestations of the Spirit?

✧ When an outsider asks about our church, do our mission and values roll off the lips of our members, with joy and an invitation to investigate what God is doing?

✧ Are we creating margins in the calendar so that members have the energy and time to be good neighbors, share their faith, and invite friends to "Come and see" (John 1:46) the Lord in the local church?

Discipleship that brings faith, economics, and work together is liberating. When the glory of God and the good of others is in view, when all facets of life are saturated with God's presence and every member of the congregation wakes up on Monday with meaning for the day, the fruit will be greater than we can imagine (Eph. 1:15–23; 3:14–21).

Liturgy and Life Rhythms

Weekly worship is built into the very fabric of creation and redemption. God's rest was not cessation of providential activity but a pause from the formative labor of the six days, as well as the model for the fourth commandment for Israel and a life principle for the body of Christ. Weekly community worship is one of the "givens" for the people of God (1 Cor. 16:1–2). The exact day of the week, time, place, style, and detailed processes will vary. The biblical call to rejoice in God's character and grace, repent and return to covenant love, receive instruction from the Word, and respond to the Spirit is the privilege of all God's people in all locales.

For some Spirit-filled Christians, the word *liturgy* evokes images of dry, formal, "religious" efforts that are dead and the opposite of lively Pentecostal worship. The word itself literally means the work of worship offered by the people of God. Any consistent times of community praise and prayer, learning and fellowship, have some kind of "liturgy." We do need the Holy Spirit to initiate, empower, and sustain all we do in response to God's amazing grace.

Community worship as obedience to the creation ordinance of the Sabbath keeps us from replacing worship of the Almighty with working for and worshipping the "almighty dollar." *Work and economics are crucial to life, but they are not all of life.* As we end the false dichotomies of sacred/secular and spiritual/practical, we need to be reminded that God is holy, transcendent, and worthy of our humble adoration for his mighty deeds and perfect character and nature (Ps. 95).

Restoring the Parish

In a world of neighborly anonymity and (pseudo) cyber intimacy, the church has a crucial countercultural and prophetic role to play in restoring a sense of place. Mass migrations, urbanization, and multicultural mobility have resulted in much dislocation in our world. During the collapse of the Western Roman Empire in the fifth century, and in recent peacemaking activities in South Africa, the church was and is the cohesive community in an atomized, fragmented world. Gathering in both large and small groups to celebrate, learn, and fellowship in covenantal renewal around the Lord's Table becomes an important touchstone for personal identity, familial connection, and missional commissioning.

Pastors as Catalysts and Equippers

Sacerdotal tasks will always be at the heart of a local leader's daily life. Prayer and service, preaching and anointing the sick, ministering grace and fostering spiritual sensitivity, are the heart of the pastoral vocation (John 10:1–18; 1 Peter 5:1–4). But the equipping task of Ephesians 4:11–16 must not be lost in the midst of other good activities. Pastors cannot be specialists in every non-theological arena. They can, however, understand the diverse fields in their parish and empower God's people with understanding the importance of their work and its connection to God's mission in the world.

Evangelization may be stimulated by vocational evangelists or gifted pastors, but the actual work is carried out by enthusiastic and well-prepared members who have learned how to share the gospel story and their personal testimony. Ephesians 4:12–16 provides indicators of effective equipping:

- ✧ All God's people are being prepared for their arenas of service.

- ✧ The body is built up, made stronger by each member's growth in grace.

- ✧ There is increasing unity and maturity.

- ✧ There is doctrinal, moral, and relational stability.

- ✧ Christ is glorified as the head of the church—the church's source and sovereign.

The challenge is clear: spiritual leaders must empower and release, and not bind and constrict the work of the Spirit.

Back-to-the-Future Moments

As we consider the church an incubator of transformation, a community that commissions the people of God as ambassadors in all their fields, some stories of impact from church history are inspiring and instructive. The following narratives illustrate something vital for our efforts in twenty-first-century discipleship. God's people have often led the way in cultural, economic, and social creativity and innovation. Our heroes of the faith, however, were not always appreciated in their time. As we consider transformation in our churches, we will face resistance. Often the leaders of the last generation's advances are the least supportive of change in the current generation.

These stories are chosen as illustrations of our five principles. From the goodness of work to social virtue, we can lead the way in both revival and reformation, in ecstatic moments and ethical ministries, and in personal and social transformation.

Benedict Puts Monks to Work
(Principles One and Three)

By the early sixth century, monastic communities were in need of reform. From the Egyptian hermits of the third century, monastic vocations had multiplied and many groups were well-organized and generously funded. Others lived in abject poverty and extreme asceticism. The quality of spiritual life, hospitality, and mission ranged from zealous to indolent, and the standards for religious life varied enormously.

Into this nadir comes Benedict of Nursia, establishing the famous monastery at Monte Cassino in 529 and composing the *Rule* that remains an inspiration for all religious orders. For our purposes, Benedict's instructions affirm the goodness of labor as well as prayer and the importance of physical health as well as sacrificial spirituality. Many Benedictine monasteries became centers of economic innovation and hospitality for the poor. Some historians credit Benedictine leaders with furthering waterwheel technology to harvest energy for food and clothing production.

More than a thousand years later, another monk, Brother Lawrence, recorded his experiences of labor and prayer in a little treatise entitled *The Practice of the Presence of God*. Brother Lawrence resented being assigned kitchen duty that hindered full-time attention to personal devotions. He discovered that the work of God in the soul is not confined to private spiritual exercises. God is working in all circumstances to sanctify believers, and intimacy with God is found in every moment.

Intimacy with God and Intensity at Work in the Twentieth Century

Twentieth-century Presbyterian missionary and literacy advocate Frank Laubach made it his life goal to be conscious of God at every moment. His diaries are full of the agony and ecstasy of this quest. His story is compelling because his passion was integrated into a very active public life, serving thousands in India and the Philippines. These exceptional examples stimulate all believers to cultivate consciousness of the Holy Spirit, allowing his leading to guide attitudes and decisions (Rom. 8; Gal. 5; cf. 1 Kings 19 and Elijah's "still small voice" [v. 12, KJV] experience).

The Merchant-Preachers (Principles One, Three, and Five)

The Waldensian movement in twelfth- and thirteenth-century France and Italy and the Lollard followers of John Wycliffe in fourteenth- and fifteenth-century England are examples of empowered laity sharing their faith without necessarily leaving "secular" vocations. Regarded as heretical church leaders, these valiant workers sought to revive apostolic simplicity, reform lax morality, and bring the gospel and scriptural texts in the vernacular to the masses. The Waldensian and Lollard bands were not initially schismatic—they were reformers who became alienated and forced to create separate institutions.

The Moravians (Principles Three and Four)

In Protestant missionary narratives, the English Baptist cobbler William Carey (1761–1834) is recognized as the "father of modern missions" and celebrated for his evangelization, social justice, and translation work in India. His objections to the predatory policies of the East India Company and advocacy for indigenous evangelical churches in India deserve great acclaim.

More than half a century before Carey felt the calling to India, an intrepid band of believers gathered on the estate of Count Nikolaus von Zinzendorf in Herrnhut, Germany and committed to world evangelization. These Moravians were descendants of the Bohemian Brethren, whose churches and institutions were destroyed in the Thirty Years' War (1618–48). Several Lutheran Pietists joined these refugees and united to experience the love of Christ and share the gospel with others. There were Danish, German, and Czech influences among the community. Long before "business-as-mission" became a buzzword, the Moravians were pioneering enterprises in service of the kingdom of God.

Evangelical Integration
(Foundations for All Five Principles)

From the late 1730s to the 1840s, multiple spiritual awakenings within Protestant Christianity called both the churched and unchurched to conversion and consecration and gave birth to multidenominational evangelicalism, with its deep passions for evangelism, global mission, and social transformation. Evangelicals came (and still come) in all shapes and sizes. High-church Anglicans were committed to the gospel and sacramental theology. Baptists and other nonconformists were equally dedicated to gospel preaching, simple ordinances, and congregational polity. Evangelicals embraced either Arminian or Calvinist theology—evangelizing together and then sparring in print over the decrees of God. Anglicans, Baptists, Congregationalists, Methodists, Presbyterians, and Quakers all found a seat at the table of religious awakening.

Evangelical spirituality and theology varies widely in each tradition, but there are critical commonalities that have remained constants for over two centuries. These include the authority of the Bible, salvation by grace through faith, a call to personal conversion and growth in grace through the spiritual disciplines, a passion for evangelism and missions, and compassion for those in need.

The revivals of this century did not divorce conversion from discipleship or discipleship from social concern. The leading orator of the eighteenth-century "great and general awakening" in England and North America, George Whitefield, was also a tireless advocate for orphans and spent considerable time raising funds for relief for the poor. John and Charles Wesley preached to multitudes, composed hymns, and organized Methodist bands, classes, and societies for discipleship. They were also staunch advocates for social reform, working hard to improve housing, water quality, education, and other conditions for the poor. "Cleanliness is next to godliness" was spoken in reference to much more than personal hygiene—it was a clarion call to care for the newly urban poor, rural miners and laborers, and others dislocated in dirty conditions. John Woolman was a prosperous eighteenth-century Quaker who incurred the wrath of many elites when he initiated multiple movements to abolish slavery. His Society of Friends eventually saw things his way, and the Quakers became leaders in working to right this demonic institution.

Charles G. Finney led revivals in the 1820s that saw nearly five hundred thousand conversions. He also made it clear that to be a Christian meant to engage in changing the world for the better. From compassion efforts to establishing the theology department at Oberlin College and allowing women to recite and share religious experiences in his classes, Finney modeled integration in the context of the nineteenth century.

Evangelicals founded multiple missionary societies, joining with the British and other Europeans in what historian Kenneth Scott Latourette called "The Great Century" (1815 to 1914) of Christian missions. Along with evangelization, church planting, and Scripture translation, evangelicals found time to confront and make attempts to ameliorate multiple social ills, from widow-burning in India to foot-binding in China.

These robust Christians affirmed the dignity of work, private property, and limited government all within a framework of biblical faith and practice. The tragedy of the later fundamentalist-modernist split in most Protestant denominations propelled theologically conservative Christians toward private efforts at human betterment, but at the cost of public disengagement.

Pentecostal Testimonies in the Twentieth Century (All Five Principles)

"Are you saved, sanctified, and filled with the Holy Ghost?" This was a frequent inquiry in early Pentecostal and holiness circles. The query contains three distinct experiences. Salvation was understood as a crisis conversion, a decisive moment when the gospel is believed and the sinner is justified. Heaven is waiting (if you stay faithful to your confession)—this builds confidence in the future. Sanctification was a specific encounter for some traditions (e.g., Church of God and Nazarene); for others it was progressive, with measureable growth (e.g., Assemblies of God and Foursquare). Holiness was the aim and a part of enjoying the third facet of God's grace: a baptism in the Holy Spirit that empowers for mission.

What were the nascent principles in this experiential theology? First, confidence in a heavenly future resulted in deep assurance. This is basic evangelical testimony. Second, sanctification brought victory over willful sin. The endless struggle of Romans 7 yields to a more positive sense of responsibility arising from the power of the Spirit in Romans 8. This carries over to the family and the workplace. Finally, the Spirit-baptism that propelled believers into the "last-days harvest fields" so they could "throw out the lifeline" and "rescue the perishing" before the rapture of the church and/or the second coming was also present to transform daily life.

Powerful conversions and consecrations united with passion for mission did not immediately translate into mature reflection on the cultural mandate of Scripture or a vocational stewardship focus. Pentecostals prized (and still prize) "the call to ministry," which has had the cumulative effect of continuing the dichotomistic thinking mentioned earlier. Yet there was a winsomeness about Spirit-filled laity feeling called by God "to be a witness at work" and a faithful worker in the church, all the while generously funding the efforts of evangelists, missionaries, and pastors, as well as the new parachurch efforts that sprang up in the second half of the twentieth century.

Most "ministry to business" took the form of groups like the Full Gospel Business Mens Fellowship International (FGBMFI), founded after World War II to provide a vehicle for Pentecostal businessmen to invite friends to breakfast and to hear an inspirational speaker on the neutral ground of a local restaurant. Similar groups continue to meet. Until the last two decades, most of the communication focused on the spiritual testimony of a prominent lay business leader.

Pentecostals are inspired pragmatists as they carry out the Great Commission. With a passion for souls, Pentecostals started schools, hospitals, addiction treatment centers (Teen Challenge), rescue missions, and vocational training centers. These were and are born in prayer and assessment of unmet needs on the ground. Pentecostals are committed to personal and social uplift and care deeply about discipleship, as converts and graduates of their programs go to work and raise families.

In the last two decades, Pentecostal leaders, concomitant with organizations such as the Acton Institute and other evangelical networks, have started to think deeply about the ideological, philosophical, and structural challenges they are confronting in their missionary efforts. In the next chapter, some extraordinary examples of integration will be presented.

Time for Real Application: Churches as Cities of Refuge Amid Turbulent Times

What if someone were to read this chapter and ask, "This sounds great, but what about job creation? If God is creative, shouldn't Christians be creative about economics and opportunities for people to work?"

What a provocative question and prophetic challenge! Instead of just praying at an altar, dispensing charity, and offering encouraging platitudes, what if local churches brought together leaders from different fields and prayed about wealth creation and economic transformation, with the tangible goal of increasing opportunity and reducing unemployment?

The results would look different in every location. Demographic, educational, environmental, and social situations will present diverse challenges and opportunities for churches to hear from God. In fact, economic needs can be a catalyst for multiple local churches to work together as an answer to the prayer of Jesus recorded in John 17, all the while being catalysts of prosperity.

Young adults entering the workforce today face new circumstances and obstacles; however, we serve a Lord who is "the same yesterday and today and forever" (Heb. 13:8). Our God delights in offering wisdom through faithful prayer (James 1:5–6); and as we seek his face, we can understand the best way forward in our work world (Phil. 1:9–11).

Older workers face crises of confidence and hope as jobs move away and industries retool for global competition. Emotional and physical health, and even lifespan, are affected by the dignity of daily work. When there is little hope or purpose and individuals move from providing well for their families to receiving charity, the consequences are often devastating.

Earlier we considered the notion that the next awakening or revival would not be led by a single leader or confined to one location. Perhaps the Fourth Great Awakening will connect spiritual renewal in Christians, the conversion of unbelievers, and discipleship that fosters job creation and the prosperity of our communities and the nation. We trust God to heal our bodies, restore our souls, and transform our relationships. Can we believe that the same sovereign Spirit can also lead humble, prayerful people to lead a flourishing economy?

Study Questions

1. When do you rest and reflect on the goodness of God? How are you practicing Sabbath in your life?
2. What are the current economic concerns in our communities? How are we equipping ourselves for the twenty-first-century economy?
3. What aspects of the Benedictine and Waldensian stories are relevant in the here and now?
4. Why do so many adults under the age of thirty-five affirm love for Jesus but feel alienated from the church?

For Further Reading

Batterson, Mark. *The Circle Maker: Praying Circles Around Your Biggest Dreams and Greatest Fears.* Grand Rapids: Zondervan, 2011.

Clarensau, Michael. *From Belonging to Becoming: The Power of Loving People Like Jesus Did.* Springfield, MO: Influence Resources, 2011.

Peterson, Eugene. *Practice Resurrection: A Conversation on Growing Up in Christ.* Grand Rapids: Eerdmans, 2010.

Webber, Robert. *Who Gets to Narrate the World? Contending for the Christian Story in an Age of Rivals.* Downers Grove, IL: InterVarsity, 2008.

The Local Church | 7

Commissioned for Impact in All Domains

I n popular parlance, are the facets of human life summarized in seven mountains, ten spheres, or a dozen domains? Profound and simplistic literature abounds sustaining all these motifs. The real biblical conviction is that Christ is Lord of all of life, no matter how we currently categorize its dimensions. Brett Johnson argues that once we ascend the "mountain of the LORD" (Isa. 2:3; Mic. 4:2) and get God's perspective on creation and redemption, all the other mountains look like molehills!

In this chapter, we will assess several dimensions of our work in the world. It is important to see "work" as more than a business transaction (though this kind of work matters). *Our work is our daily life lived as an offering to God.*

Dave Buehring, author of the recently released *The Jesus Blueprint*, argues that discipleship is no more and no less than infusing the character, nature, and ways of God in every domain. We have established that the work of God takes place through work and active participation in the welfare of the community and nation. Economic thriving is a driver (though not the only one) that helps propel advances in other domains. Let's examine the diverse arenas of God's kingdom activity and connect them with the empowerment of the Spirit and economic flourishing.

The Great Commandment and a Vision of a New Normal

When our Lord tells us that all the Law and the Prophets hang on the commandments to love God and neighbor (Matt. 22:37–40), it is imperative that we understand the full implications of what this means. When we love God, we will begin to be more comfortable in our own skin (personal wholeness) and we will allow his presence to change us from the inside out (Eph. 4:22–24). Security with God and a healthy self-image empower us to be intentional about healthy and wise relationships with others (relational integrity). Obedience to the revealed will of God in these basic arenas opens us to awareness of God's specific plans for us (John 8:31–32), and we start fulfilling our purpose with precision (vocational clarity).

God's Business

Discipleship is about connections, integration, and all the threads of life being woven together into a beautiful tapestry. In the parable of the talents in Matthew 25:14–30, the master left varying amounts of money with his servants and expected a return. Of course, the application of Jesus' parable is not confined to financial gain; it refers to proper stewardship of the abilities, opportunities, and relationships of each believer.

Being a follower of Christ is the most amazing business deal imaginable. God gives us natural and supernatural gifts. The Holy Spirit lives in us. The Word of God is open to us. We are in fellowship with wise and encouraging believers. Opportunities to witness and work are before us every day. All we need to do is invest God's resources and depend upon the Holy Spirit—and we will be rewarded. What a wonderful partnership. God does all the "heavy lifting" through the work of Christ and through his patience with us as we learn to use his gifts. Our task is to take God's resources and watch them multiply.

A New Look at Isaiah 61

Of course there is labor—God calls us as his cocreators and partners in his restoring, rebuilding, and renewing works. These three verbs—*restore*, *rebuild*, and *renew*—are found in Isaiah 61. The first few verses of this chapter are well-known because Jesus inaugurated his public ministry with an exposition of the opening verses, declaring their fulfillment in his hometown synagogue (Luke 4:16–21). Christian scholars usually assign the later verses to the future millennial or eternal reign of Christ. Complete rebuilding, renewing, and restoring remains in the future, concomitant with the second coming. But the kingdom of God is living the future now in the power of the Holy Spirit, with our efforts as significant signposts of the future. With this mindset, creativity and thoughtfulness of all facets of human flourishing can be unleashed to all who "seek first the kingdom of God" (Matt. 6:33).

PROFILE IN COURAGE

Ken Janke and Groundworks, New Haven, Connecticut

Ken Janke spent most of his adult life as an evangelist, pastor, and church planter. As part of his desire to evangelize and bless the city of New Haven, his mission has expanded in recent years. In a world of brokenness, alienation, and economic and racial division, Groundworks seeks to bring healing and hope, reconciliation and redemption, by presenting an integrated vision of community health. They have a new facility called The Grove, where multiple businesses and nonprofit organizations share space and vision.

Ken's aim is evangelization *and* the transformation of New Haven: one relationship, one neighborhood, one new business at a time. There is an integration of the worlds of ministry and work, worship and witness, service and spiritual growth, that is refreshing and all too rare. Business development cannot be separated from community service. Church growth must not be isolated from social transformation. Personal flourishing and political wholeness are connected in God's kingdom.

Public officials often speak of rebuilding physical infrastructure—bridges, roads, and sewers—as part of their stewardship responsibility. This is good and necessary work. But the moral, relational, and spiritual foundations need rebuilding and maintaining as well. God's people aim to restore the whole person and the entire culture.

Welcoming the Holy Spirit

For nearly two thousand years, Christians have prayed, "Come, Holy Spirit." Pentecostals are renewed as they sing and cry out, "Holy Spirit, you are welcome in this place." The personal and communal experience of the manifest presence of the Holy Spirit is the desire of all devout Christians. The mature believer will offer these same prayers outside the walls of the church, within the context of every activity. (Prayers for parking spaces and short lines in governmental offices are not in view here!)

"Come, Holy Spirit" is an invitation for God to help business leaders make wise decisions about resources, marketing, and personnel. "Come, Holy Spirit" is the prayer of a devout mother looking for the best ways to nurture her child's gifts and restrain the destructive impulses ready to subvert progress. This same prayer is the heart cry of many doctors—such as David Levy (author of *Gray Matter*, a recent work on prayer and medical care), as he performs exacting brain surgery.

When we welcome the Holy Spirit, we are welcoming the assurance of the Father that we are his children (Gal. 3:26—4:7). We are welcoming Christ in all his fullness. Jesus is Lord and "lover of my soul." Christ is King and Friend. He is the firstborn—through his resurrection—among many brothers and sisters (Rom. 8:29; Col. 1:18). We are welcoming God's sovereignty as we humbly submit to the voice of the Lord in the texts of the Bible, the insights of mature leaders, the historic communion of saints, the present manifestations of the Spirit, and the common grace of other astute voices. Fellow leader, it is vital that God's people learn how to "hear"—opening their spiritual ears to the frequency of faith that will inform every dimension of their world (Eph. 3:14–19).

Some Exemplary Domains of Discipleship

Flourishing churches and communities will impact a variety of areas of life, depending upon the constituents of the community and the unique qualifiers of place and time. Here is just a sampling of what happens when integration becomes normal and we welcome the Holy Spirit.

Family Life: Modeling Triune Love

Work takes place in the home and neighborhood, with or without an official "wage." Unpaid, volunteer service is still work. When led by the Spirit, it "counts" as kingdom service. A parent choosing to raise children, tend the home, and volunteer at church and school is fulfilling a divine calling just as much as a pastor preparing a sermon or an executive closing a corporate merger.

Family life embraces the quality of marital maturity as spouses learn to love and serve each other, pray effectively, and support each other's vocations. An often overlooked dimension of marriage is the fact that couples have callings that transcend and unite their individual expressions. Every Christian couple can answer the question, "Why did we marry?" with more than general answers. The biblical purposes for all marriages are honorable and need to be affirmed; covenantal worship, mutual delight, bearing the next generation (for most), and mutual support are foundational. But the Holy Spirit longs to impart specific insights to each couple, if the partners will humbly listen.

Consider John and Mary, for example. John is a sales executive and Mary is an elementary school teacher, and together they are raising two rambunctious boys. They serve their church faithfully. They support each other's vocations, including the economic and time sacrifice of each spouse earning an advanced degree. They welcome the Holy Spirit into all facets of work and play. In other words, they are happy and healthy, an exemplary couple by all reasonable standards.

Though nothing is wrong with this picture, more color and dimension will be added to their canvas as John and Mary inquire of the Lord together. One night as they are praying, they are led to get involved in literacy programs that help young and old learn to read and foster a desire to learn. They see this as a prerequisite for a larger undertaking: helping their fellow church members and other friends become biblically literate. They don't leave their jobs, stop parenting well, or depart from other arenas of service. They now have a task in which they are partners and need the help of others in the community.

At this stage in their journey, John and Mary's "couple calling" is framed by their delight in reading Augustine's *Confessions*.

They love the passage where the famous saint was drawn to "take up and read" the Holy Scriptures and experienced conversion and cleansing by the sovereign work of God. Mary and John are excited to help many people take up and read God's Word and discover the same transforming power of the Spirit.

The family is God's idea and reflects the very life of the Trinity. The Father loves the Son and the Son loves the Father, with the Holy Spirit as the uncreated bond of this intimate relation. Divine love created the universe and humankind. Human love creates the next generation. The joyful fellowship of the Trinity is reflected in Jesus' willing submission to the Father, the Father's affirmation of Christ's uniqueness, and the Holy Spirit's confirmation of this truth in the hearts of multitudes. A family living in love brings out the best in character and mission as all the family members find their place in God's plan.

Business and Commerce:
More Than Funding "Spiritual" Activities

God in Christ has sanctified the world of work, including all facets of business and commerce. The Holy Spirit is just as active on the factory floor as he is in a prayer meeting—if Christians are listening. There is an ever-increasing body of literature on honoring God at work. This is a positive development. A sense of calling, biblical ethics, relational integrity, spiritual sensitivity, and professional skill are all part of work as worship.

In the world of business and commerce, all Christian workers, no matter where they are in the chain of command of a particular entity, need to view themselves as "God's contractors" and be liberated to excellence, freedom, and integrity. From receptionist to researcher, custodian to CEO, all Christians are on loan from God to the world and will give an account to the Lord for the quality of their efforts. This doesn't mean that believers cannot be full-time-with-benefits employees or that they should capitulate to narcissism and think they are "God's gift" to the company and superior to their peers.

"God's contractor," in this context, is an effective way to call attention to the appropriate biblical term: steward—which is at the same time both humbling (God is the owner) and noble (we are entrusted with resources). Since "God opposes the proud but gives grace to the humble" (James 4:6; 1 Peter 5:5), Christians with this disposition and discipline can expect dynamic insights and strength from the Holy Spirit as they carry out their daily tasks (Rom. 8; Gal. 5) into new avenues of wealth creation and, in the words of Howard K. Snyder, are at the forefront of fashioning new economic and social ecosystems that consider immediate gain and long-term stewardship. Good environmental policy means resources for wealth creation for generations to come. Being caretakers of God's world includes both creation care and economic development. Environmental sensitivity makes good economic sense. The Greek term for stewardship, *oikonomia*, embraces both management and innovation.

PROFILE IN COURAGE

Business Success and Strategic Philanthropy:
The Green Family

The Green family, Pentecostal believers from Oklahoma, have founded several companies and strategically donated hundreds of millions of dollars to Christian ministries. What makes them distinct from other commendable Christian philanthropists is their conscientious biblical reflection on all facets of their work. Early in their business ventures, the family exemplified the highest Christian ethics toward their customers and employees, including offering jobs to the physically challenged. Well-known enterprises Hobby Lobby (founded by David Green) and Mardel Christian stores (founded by son Mart) are part of the Green family's vast network of business concerns. In 2005, Mart was named one of Christian retailing's Top Fifty People of the last fifty years. His motto is "This Book is Alive," and all his ventures exemplify the integration of biblical principles with excellent, relevant impact.

One of Mart's efforts is EthnoGraphic Media. Its purpose is "to serve by sharing true stories that take on the most difficult subjects." Films on HIV/AIDS, the conflict between Israelis and Palestinians, and other sensitive subjects have been well-received. Mart is also engaged in transforming the movie industry, one good film at a time. He modestly speaks of "finding the right people," and he founded Every Tribe Entertainment, which produced the critically acclaimed *End of the Spear*. This set a new standard for quality family films that are infused with a Christian worldview.

The Green family has recently revolutionized the fiscal strength and leadership structure of Oral Roberts University. Always a solid academic and spiritual community, ORU was in desperate need of infrastructure overhaul. After donations totaling over one hundred million dollars and Mart's leadership as chairman of the board, ORU is poised for global impact in the twenty-first century. The false dichotomies of business versus ministry and secular work versus the mission field are transformed into an ethos of service.

The Forgotten Workers: Factory and Field Personnel, Day Laborers, and Service Providers

Throughout history, most people have spent most of their time literally earning their daily bread. In the past two centuries, industrialization and computerization have transformed the world and created enormous wealth, social change, and human challenges.

Most Christian resources on Business as Mission (BAM) and the Theology of Work (TOW) do an excellent job—for those with the status and time to reflect on the economy and work. The conferences and literature focus on leadership and wealth creation.

The entrepreneur—large or small—is the focus, from recipients of microlending in Bangladesh to the founders of large corporate enterprises employing thousands.

Often lost in analysis are the millions who labor at backbreaking, dirty, repetitive jobs that, in the words of Mike Rowe, "make civilized life possible." I wrote this book using a computer that was likely made in a factory where thousands of people work for daily wages. The lunch I ate today included salad ingredients picked by workers in a hot field. From making cars to clothing, from cooking to plumbing, from gardening to home repair, we must remember that *all* work matters to God. All work has inherent value, but that doesn't mean all work is enjoyable in the moment or full of profound meaning to the person exhausted by a day's labor.

Discipleship that integrates faith, work, and economics must consider the efforts of those who keep the engines of commerce working and labor to feed our nation and the world. Here are some insights for those who will rarely speak at conferences or capture the attention of the media:

⋄ Honest, hard work has inherent dignity and is important to the economy—therefore, it is a vital part of God's work in the world (principle one).

⋄ Sweat and toil are a result of the fall, but they also feed the world; and those who work in factories and fields are part of God's provision (principle two).

⋄ Factory, field, and service work often open doors for conversations that become evangelism opportunities. The joy of the Lord and a heart of service will impress the most callous hearts (principle three).

⋄ When a laborer seeks the Lord, he or she has access to the same Holy Spirit that bestows wisdom upon a CEO or scientific researcher. God will give the humble seeker

insights that lead to innovative ways at work. Will we
"tune in" to God's presence while at work?

✧ There may be moments in which God will use a worker to
promote justice at the job site and in the community. It is
imperative that spiritual leaders listen to the experiences
of all of God's people, not just public elites.

The Creative Arts

Pentecostals are known for expressive worship and dynamic music. In recent decades the visual arts have started to come back into
focus, but there is much work to be done. The historical combination of puritanical iconoclasts, leaders who see the arts as dens
of iniquity, and a weak theology of culture have all contributed
to current ignorance and fear. With the infusion of charismatic
Christians from other cultural traditions and the connectedness
of global media, the landscape is changing and many communities
are encouraging artistic creativity.

There is a great need for empowerment in the arts and for
Christians to offer beauty in place of artificial images. This does
not imply saccharine work that ignores human depravity and
suffering. We must provide cultural leadership, with Christians
offering quality work joined with an eternal message—forging admirable creations that point to the triune God.

PROFILE IN COURAGE

Makoto Fujimura: Awakening the Arts

Perhaps once a century or so, a unique figure graces the world with
new eyes. Such may be the legacy of Makoto Fujimura. An accomplished artist, his works adorn galleries and museums around the

world. In 1992 Fujimura founded the International Arts Movement (IAM), a community of artists integrating faith and art and reflecting deeply on beauty and truth. Fujimura is also a writer, with his 2009 book, *Refractions: A Journey of Faith, Art and Culture*, setting a standard for fresh thinking. He was a presidential appointee to the National Council on the Arts from 2003–2009.

In celebration of the four-hundredth anniversary of the King James Bible in 2001, Crossway published *The Four Holy Gospels* (ESV), featuring Fujimura's illuminations of the sacred texts. In endorsing this project, Pastor Tim Keller of Redeemer Presbyterian Church in New York City stated, "According to Christian theology, the Illuminator is the Holy Spirit, and therefore I believe from what I can see that the Illuminator has illuminated the illuminator."

Fujimura is a model of focus and integration. He knows his calling as an artist and understands the larger context into which the arts find their expression. He unabashedly calls the church to holy, joyful, and loving reflection on the arts. He also calls Christians to repent of their cultural obscurity and stop excusing poor work by declaring it to be spiritual.

Leaders, what would happen if our churches became centers of cultural renewal? Imagine a call for artists to offer their interpretations of an upcoming sermon series, especially during Advent or Lent. A juried art exhibit would establish the parish as a hospitable place for exploration and thoughtfulness. People who would rarely darken the doors of a church will come for a quality cultural event. Leadership here involves creative literature, performing arts, and visual arts, and an openness to the Spirit to hear new global songs of worship in the many tongues that make their way to the parish.

The Sciences

Until the late nineteenth and early twentieth centuries, scientific progress and Christian faith were—with a few exceptions (e.g., Galileo)—synchronous, with empirical discoveries revealing the complexities of creation and new technologies improving the human condition. Then along came Darwin, and especially his ideological disciples who took his theories and made them into a pseudo religion. The fundamentalist-modernist split embodied in the Scopes Trial of 1925 created a dichotomy that is only recently being healed through valiant efforts of scientific and theological leaders.

PROFILE IN COURAGE

Francis Collins

Francis Collins, author of *The Language of God* and a pioneer in mapping the human genome, represents all that is salutary about full Christian engagement in the sciences. He not only affirms Christian truth but leads his discipline and participates in the crucible of private and public research and development that offers great hope for overcoming debilitating diseases. Having thoughtful leaders like Collins is vital to ensuring biblical boundaries for ethical practices and the proper relationship between the disciplines of science and theology. We don't want clerical leaders confined to the Rock of Ages while scientists affirm the ages of the rocks. Scientific inquiry is serious business, and Christians should be unafraid to explore the macrocosms and microcosms of God's world.

Two years ago, Francis Collins spoke about Christian faith at Stanford University. Several students became followers of Christ and were baptized in the months following Collins's presentation.

Communication and Media

In less than a century we have seen exponential growth in the amount and immediacy of knowledge accessible to billions of people. We have evolved (or, as philosopher Thomas Kuhn put it, made quantum leaps or paradigm shifts) from live speeches and print media containing news days or weeks old to instant awareness of events on the other side of our planet. It may be another century before we comprehend the full impact of this change and its effects on the human psyche.

Leaving aside current American-centric debates on media and ideology, what does a kingdom vocation in this field look like, with such potential to utilize it for good or ill? The Holy Spirit is "the Spirit of truth" (John 14:17; 15:26; 16:13), eschewing human fabrication and unwise speculation (Col. 2:4–8). Christian communication and media leaders will be truthful and distinguish facts from speculation and casual opinion from carefully reasoned reflection.

Christian callings in communication and media are breaking out of stereotypical religious programming and the rare testimony of integrity among secular media. Biblical faith removes craven fear and empowers dauntless pursuit of the heart of any matter. The presence of the Holy Spirit also enables the believer to test the spirits and discern the presence of extraordinary evil or special grace. Piety is never an excuse for shoddy or shallow effort.

Christian engagement in this domain unites passionate conviction with critical thinking. Journalism does not confuse organized presentation of available facts (with openness to correction as more information becomes available) with either considered or off-the-cuff opinions. Robust theology creates analytical and investigative stability—the facts of any matter are no threat to a sovereign God. Clear affirmation of both human depravity and human dignity creates categories for evaluation and understanding. In the same day, humankind witnesses unspeakable horrors initiated by twisted individuals and unimaginable acts of goodness performed by anonymous saints.

Education and Intellectual Leadership

American historian and evangelical thought leader Mark Noll has written extensively on the failure of modern evangelicals to assume places of intellectual leadership in the academy and society. Fundamentalist reactions to the hijacking of seminaries and universities at the end of the nineteenth and early twentieth centuries created new institutions that were designed to shield developing minds from the poisons of liberalism and secularism while ensuring proper Bible training for vocational ministry. While this process was and is historically understandable, Noll calls on evangelicals to pursue academic and intellectual leadership and discover that biblical faith is not threatened by secular attacks.

Pentecostal Christians do face an uphill battle in this arena. We must not only confront thinkers hostile to the gospel, but we also face fellow Christians who are contemptuous—or at least skeptical—that Pentecostals have anything to offer other than evangelical thoughts recycled by those who speak in tongues.

One realm that must come back under our purview is public education. There is a place for homeschooling and parochial education. But fear must not be the ruling consideration when it comes to parental decisions and professional callings. And some individuals and families will no doubt be called to serve on the local school board, evaluate textbooks, or develop curriculum.

Education and a calling to intellectual leadership place believers on the frontiers of thinking, which is threatening to religious mindsets that have syncretized ideological frameworks with their confessional theology (i.e., that have mixed political opinions uncritically with religious loyalties). Conversely, the academic and public intellectual world are quite entrenched, with their own Mt. Olympus of cognitive deities, patron saints, and safe frameworks from which they can hurl condescending insults toward the uninitiated.

On a practical note, Bethel Church of San Jose (mentioned in the preface, "Scotty's Story") and many other Silicon Valley churches are finding real favor as they serve local schools. From after-school clubs, to service projects, to expert help in needed areas, opportunities abound. Building positive relationships with local educators and families and helping where needed is opening doors for the gospel without untimely proselytizing. These partnerships are productive, and people are coming to Christ because believers are giving their time with love and wisdom.

PROFILES IN COURAGE

William Pickthorn and Gordon Fee

These two men are placed together because they were intellectual and spiritual pioneers within the evangelical and Pentecostal worlds. William Pickthorn was one of the first Assemblies of God ministers to obtain graduate education in religion from a secular university, receiving an MA from Stanford in the 1950s. At the time, many of his peers feared for his soul as he interacted with mainline leaders and liberal scholars. William learned much, witnessed consistently, and developed his apologetics skills, as well as integrated the disciplines of psychology and theology. He was one of the pioneers in the charismatic renewal, helping establish several "Christian Center" churches that served people of all backgrounds.

Gordon Fee is respected globally for his New Testament scholarship, particularly his studies in Paul's Christology and pneumatology and his magisterial commentary on First Corinthians. He was one of the NIV translators and served several colleges and seminaries in his distinguished career. Fee and Pickthorn were passionate in their spirituality—equally at home in prayer and healing meetings as well as libraries and classrooms. They represent the best in irenic Pentecostal Christianity and intellectual rigor.

Fellow leader, will you challenge your congregants to think deeply and act decisively? Will you be a catalyst for new thought leaders in your community, supporting efforts to consider seriously what it means to form a Christian perspective on a given issue?

Social Justice

The moment the term "social justice" is uttered, sparks fly. The Oikonomia Network document "Theology That Works" makes a strong biblical case for Christian leadership in the world of work as essential for generating the resources that lead to equitable living conditions and widespread human flourishing.

No thoughtful Christian is "against" social justice per se. What is disconcerting is the way the term has degenerated into a rallying cry for ideologues. For Christians, justice is part of God's reign and includes covenantal honesty, personal integrity, the rule of law, and compassion for those beset by misfortune.

Though the engagement of the church in tangible charity and moral advocacy is admirable, it needs to grow in scope. In the midst of this righteous activity, we must not commit the critical "either/or" fallacy. Economic development *and* compassionate sharing of resources are compatible. Free markets *and* the rule of law are essential for liberty and opportunity.

PROFILE IN COURAGE

John Wesley's "Social Ethics"

John Wesley and his brother Charles were the founders of the Methodist movement and central to the birth of the evangelical movement in England and America that has propelled global Protestant missions for two and a half centuries. As he led people to faith in Christ and developed discipleship processes, Wesley and his fellow Methodists worked tirelessly for social reform. There were no gaps between personal conversion/renewal and moral/practical service to one's neighbor.

Wesley scholar Sondra Wheeler puts it this way: "John Wesley didn't have 'social ethics.' I say that because both of the distinctions implied in that term—the distinction between social and personal ethics and the distinction between ethics and theology—are alien to Wesley's thought and to his life" (see "The Project on Lived Theology" at www .livedtheology.org).

How did Wesley promote social justice? During his busy evangelistic career, he and his followers led campaigns for the poor and exposed the corruptions of the rich—especially those in public office. They supported fair prices, living wages, clean housing, and education, while affirming property rights, personal liberties, and scientific/technological innovation. Methodists believed in gradual, persuasive reform that first had to be embodied in individual and church actions before spreading to the rest of society. And they did all of this while experiencing the power of the Spirit—so much so that some historians designate them as "proto-Pentecostals."

Civil, Political, and Military Service

For the past several decades Pentecostals have joined other evangelicals in rediscovering civil and military leadership as a kingdom calling. The Assemblies of God Theological Seminary (AGTS) trains a large number of institutional and military chaplains. Many opponents of the gospel are complaining that the military chaplaincy is too Christian, and there have been calls for watering down public prayers and marginalizing devout Christians.

From the progressive Evangelicals for Social Action (founded in 1973) to the conservative Moral Majority (founded in 1979), a variety of Christian organizations have been working for both broad and narrow causes, including pro-life concerns, legal defenses of religious liberty, and electing ethical public officials.

When offered to God, all legitimate work is service; and this applies especially to elected officials. Politicians are not only stewards of their personal resources—they have a public trust to serve the populace with integrity and wisdom. In ideologically polarized cultures, Christian peacemaking is an active, Spirit-empowered discipline that leads to sociocultural progress. Imagine Christians of all backgrounds praying and working for real-life solutions to public issues without regard to partisanship and media sound bites. Military service will be debated until Jesus returns. In a fallen world, fresh articulation of just war theory and vigorous advocacy for all nonviolent options are critical priorities.

Health, Medicine, and Wholeness

Throughout history Christians have been at the forefront of caring for the sick, believing in both natural and supernatural solutions to human infirmities. Our modern hospitals grew out of monastic hospitality and Christian civic responsibility. Christian compassion that leads to care for the vulnerable—from orphans to widows, from the wounds of war to wounds of body and psyche—is something all believers can be proud of.

Christian care by definition is holistic, nurturing all aspects of human existence, without religious coercion. The integration of physical, spiritual, emotional, and social realities contributes greatly to healing. The kingdom call to repentance and reconciliation in the context of eucharistic celebration is an often overlooked facet of Christian experience that contributes to health. Unforgiveness and willful resistance to the Spirit in community relationships imperil physical as well as spiritual health (1 Cor. 10–11).

PROFILE IN COURAGE

David Levy and the Integration of Faith and Medical Care

Dr. David Levy is an adult convert to the Christian faith and a talented neurosurgeon. What makes his medical practice exemplary is his habit of requesting to pray for his patients as part of his care.

If they refuse, he still offers the best care he can; and his surgical successes have earned him an excellent reputation. If permission is granted, Levy prays with patients and urges them to consider the connections of their emotional, relational, spiritual, and physical being.

Some patients have miraculous recoveries; others do not. But all of Dr. Levy's patients and their families testify to the excellent personal and professional care they receive.

This example does not mean that Christians can inappropriately insert religious activity into any circumstances of work and service. Discernment and discretion are needed (though silent prayer is always a good choice), as the seeds of the kingdom grow into fruitful places of nourishment.

It All Comes Back to Stewardship

When we stand before the "judgment seat of Christ" (2 Cor. 5:10), our efforts to serve God in this age will come under divine scrutiny. There is much speculation concerning the "fire" that will "test the quality of each man's work" (1 Cor. 3:13). Uniting these two texts with Jesus' parables of the workers in the vineyard and the talents (Matt. 20:1–16; 25:14–30), a clearer picture emerges regarding God's evaluation of our work.

All Christians are saved by grace, and no one enjoying the eternal presence of God will take any credit for their status. "Worthy is the Lamb!" is the only refrain we can say before a holy God who has shown us such mercy.

What we do get to say to our Lord is, "Look, Master, what you gave me—your Holy Spirit, gifts, opportunities, relationships, and resources—they yielded good fruit in others as I put them to use. Here is what you did through my humble efforts."

G. O. Forde once said that the good works believers will be rewarded for are the ones we have forgotten about. Unselfish and unselfconscious service for the glory of God and the good of others is the aim. Making lasting contributions to flourishing churches and communities counts before God. In the parables, the master does not distinguish between "secular" and "spiritual" work—no such dichotomy exists for the Almighty! The challenge for us is fidelity to our faith and worship through our work.

Study Questions

1. In what domains/mountains/spheres are you serving? What are some of God's current instructions as you live for Christ in the midst of hostility and indifference?

2. Why are the fine arts controversial for followers of Christ?

3. What are some principles that should guide Christian participation in government and military service?

4. What "social justice" issues affect people in your local church?

For Further Reading

Buehring, Dave. *The Jesus Blueprint: Rediscovering His Original Plan for Changing the World.* Oviedo, FL: HigherLife Publishing, 2012.

Fujimura, Makoto. *Refractions: A Journey of Faith, Art and Culture.* Colorado Springs: NavPress, 2009.

Johnson, Brett. *Ministry of Business Bible Study.* Saratoga, CA: The Institute for Innovation, Integration & Impact, 2011.

———. Transforming Society: A Framework for Fixing a Broken World. Saratoga, CA: Indaba Publishing, 2010.

Keller, Tim. *Center Church: Doing Balanced, Gospel-Centered Ministry in Your City.* Grand Rapids: Zondervan, 2012.

Levy, David. *Gray Matter: A Neurosurgeon Discovers the Power of Prayer . . . One Patient at a Time.* Carol Stream, IL: Tyndale, 2011.

Noll, Mark. Jesus Christ and the Life of the Mind. Grand Rapids: Eerdmans, 2011.

Conclusion

Discovery, Integration, and New Measures of Success

We are at the end of a revolutionary call to integrate faith, work, and economics. Our minds are challenged; our hearts are stirred by the many testimonies of Spirit-filled believers making a difference for the Lord in all the arenas of work and the economy. We want to act—but where do we begin? This vision is not just another sermon series or set of programs. That is a relief, in light of the inundation of information we face every day.

But we have lessons and sermons to prepare. There are people in crisis that need immediate attention. Recruiting and refreshing volunteers is a never-ending task. Mobilizing current leaders around our new purpose, vision, mission, values, and strategic plan takes huge amounts of energy. Just getting folks to pray and read their Bibles, tithe, and show up to help is daunting, along with the challenge to present sound doctrine and to battle the constant comparisons with celebrities in the Christian media.

Here is the good news: *This new integration is not another sermon series, set of meetings, or new list of programs. Discipleship that connects faith, work, and economics is an adventure of faith.* Remember, the Holy Spirit resides in each member and in the gathered community, ready to guide us as we humbly walk in the fear of the Lord and mutual respect for one another. God's Word declares that "we have the mind of Christ" (1 Cor. 2:16) and can "discern what is best" (Phil. 1:10). The stories in Acts—as doors opened and closed, prophecies and visions guided the apostles (Acts 13; 16; 20)—inspire our faith in God's power to lead his church. James reminds us that God delights in generously giving wisdom to those who believe (James 1:5–6) and are willing to live out the relational and social implications (James 3:13–18). Romans 8 and Galatians 5 stir us to character growth and moment-by-moment reliance on the Lord as we "keep in step with the Spirit."

Three insights will help propel our steps forward.

Insight One: Discovery

The path forward begins with discovering how God is already at work in our situation. This awakening to the current work of the Spirit has several facets—none of which immediately adds to our to-do list. As a reminder of what we covered in earlier chapters and as a way of putting our faith into action, let's consider the following discoveries.

Once we have done our cultural exegesis and learned the cultural, demographic, economic, social, and spiritual realities of our target community, we are ready to ask the question, "How do we see God's common grace at work around us, from neighbors who care for each other to businesses that are ready to grow? How is God demonstrating his goodness in the everyday lives of the people we are called to reach for the Lord?" It is easy to see the pathologies arising from sin and the needs that come in the wake of a fallen world. Sometimes we need a new set of lenses to see potential as well as problems.

Our congregants are already gifted, working hard, and trying to connect the dots. As we empower them with biblical teaching for personal wholeness, relational integrity, and vocational clarity, a tapestry of talent emerges that we can connect with our field of service and thus help those around us to flourish. Our discoveries here are all the ways the Lord has sovereignly arranged the members of the body not only to participate in the gathered worshiping community but also to contribute substantially to the economic and social transformation of the region in which they live. For example, a property owner might create a new nonprofit and open some housing to people in transition from dependency to productivity. A business owner looks for ways to expand and create jobs. These two men would normally talk about church programs or fishing; now they are connecting to get people off welfare and working again—without creating a new church program.

Life is more than for-profit activity. One of our discoveries includes connecting our members with worthy causes already serving people well. Like Pastor Valci's church in Dublin, California, we can deploy Spirit-empowered emissaries to existing agencies. This is a strategy that Earl and Janet Creps are following in their new "360 church" in Berkeley, California. Berkeley is the epitome of cultural creativity and social consciousness. Creating one more parallel program will have little impact; "seeding" current service agencies with on-fire Christians, however, is yielding good relational and spiritual fruit.

As we listen to the Lord in prayer, new images and words, connections and opportunities, will flood our hearts. Jesus promised his followers "the unforced rhythms of grace" and "a real rest" (Matt. 11:28–29 The Message) as part of the call to take up our cross daily and follow him (Luke 9:23). The powerful paradox here is that when we cease from our own humanly engineered efforts and really listen, we will find God's "good, pleasing and perfect will" in our context (Rom. 12:2).

Insight Two: Integration

As one of the leaders of your congregation, you are an important storyteller for your church family. Listening to God, the world around you, and the prayers and stories of your members provides you with an understanding of the divine narrative being written in the place and time in which you are living. Integration is no more or no less the weaving together of stories that converge as people come to Christ and enjoy life together. The four kinds of stories are: 1) God's grand redemptive narrative in Scripture; 2) God's current work in the world; 3) the story of our community and God's activity; and 4) the personal story of each believer as they awaken to God's grace, come to Christ, and commence a life of discipleship. Integration is implied in the discovery insight.

Connecting spiritual growth with all facets of life is a never-ending task, but one that must be diligently pursued. As mentioned earlier, the Bible never disconnects spiritual growth from personal character and relational health. Put bluntly, ecstasy must be united with ethics. Moments of supernatural manifestation without accompanying maturation leave a wake of dissatisfaction, with the immature addicted to experience and the thoughtful inoculated against certain phenomena.

Integration is the aha moment that happens when God's people realize they are directly connected with the current and future flourishing of the world around them and that such goodness is an integral part of the Great Commission. As a leader, you have the honor of commissioning the saints to their daily tasks with this deeper understanding. This connection includes household stewardship of the fruits of work. In addition to giving, saving, and wise spending habits, God's people need to see that their discretionary resources also matter, from supporting the arts to supporting recreation that furthers the economic prosperity of others.

An Important Pause for Reflection

How do we integrate all these insights and principles while remaining passionate about the Great Commission in light of the imminent return of the Lord Jesus Christ? Though Pentecostals argue about the details of biblical prophecy, our movement was born in a context of urgency and there is concern among many that such passion is being dissipated as we focus on "worldly" concerns. The answer? Good theology.

The next great event in God's redemptive narrative is the return of Christ. In the meantime, believers are urged to remain alert, faithful, hopeful, and well-occupied in our callings. Here is the theological key that unlocks practical integration.

With the help of the Holy Spirit, we are living the future now, with all our efforts in all domains being signposts of the future. Our eternal destiny includes worship and work in redeemed (but real) bodies, united with the entire community of saints. Our future includes gazing upon the magnificent triune God and going about meaningful tasks. In other words, we are rehearsing for our future.

Yes, the salvation of one sinner brings joy to heaven and the priority of evangelization must never be superseded. This book is about us becoming intentional about flourishing churches and communities that demonstrate the future as a witness to the truth of Christ.

Understanding Work

My thrust has been to present foundational knowledge and insight on discipleship that seamlessly integrates the worlds of weekly worship and weekly work. For most of humankind, life is work punctuated by moments of leisure and rest. This work may be creative or repetitive, well-regarded or rarely noticed, but it is all part of God's common grace and is worthy of reflection.

Work takes place both inside and outside the home. Parenting is work. So is the world of commerce. Serious artistic efforts are work. A competitive athlete trains for hours apart from public performance; that is work. Diverse cultures place different values on various kinds of work. From a Christian viewpoint, it is scandalous that the annual salaries of women and men who risk their lives for our medical and safety needs represent a fraction of what professional athletes are paid to play one or two games. Before we rush to judgment, however, both history and intelligent reflection tell us that free markets are better in the long run than command and control economies, and natural pricing and wages serve the common good better than artificially fixed levels. That said, a free society must be a virtuous one; and how we serve those who serve us says much about our values.

This effort is a call to a revolution in practical theology. It is time for followers of Christ to catch up to the words and works of Jesus and the apostles and affirm the priesthood of all believers, including the divine sanction of all legitimate vocations. This is not a call to "Christian anarchy" (an oxymoron). Ecclesial structures need not be dismantled and clerical and religious vocations need not be abandoned. All vocations are elevated. Clergy are finally released to their biblical roles as ministry-multipliers: encouraging, equipping, and empowering all people to fulfill their callings. Nonclerical church members are not second-class citizens of the religious world. They are released to Spirit-empowered positions of leadership in all spheres of civilizational work.

Loving All Seven Days

This perspective does not mean life is easy or that a believer will wake up every day with unbounded energy. If we view

life as a "Thank you!" to God for his grace in Christ;

and work as a calling;

all activity as a signpost of the future kingdom;

and the presence of the Holy Spirit as welcomed at work;

the means are the end and relationships matter;

and others see the wellsprings of contentment and joy.

Then we are beginning to love all seven days and "apprehend that for which also [we are] apprehended of Christ" (Phil. 3:12 KJV).

One of the consequences of embracing this vision is that church communities can engage with local business, education, social services, and other religious leaders to foster community wholeness. A healthy economy, safe living conditions, solid education, and mutual assistance are unquestionable facets of common grace and will build bridges for apostolic witness faster than many religious activities.

Multiple Roles with One Set of Rules

One of the unfortunate consequences of disintegrated living is the double standard of ethics and professional excellence applied to businesses and nonprofit organizations. Business leaders often scoff at the poor practices of charities and religious organizations, agitating for the infusion of best practices on their church boards. Churches and other nonprofits use limited funds or kinder ethics as excuses for poor administration or low-performing personnel. Both groups get nervous when there is talk of "more business in the church" or "bringing God to work."

There is no room in God's kingdom for such falsehood. One set of rules applies to all followers of Jesus Christ, whether they are leading a large business concern or a small parish. Yes, there are psychosocial dynamics that differ in mobilizing volunteers and evaluating paid employees. However, the same fruit of the Spirit

(Gal. 5:22–23) applies to all relationships, and the manifestations of the Spirit (1 Cor. 12–14) are not confined to parish halls and sanctuaries.

For-profit businesses are service providers. Customers place value on the goods, services, and insights companies provide. A business thrives or perishes based on how well they serve customers. The motives for Christian business include profits, for they are a measure of service excellence and a reward to all engaged in helping others. Churches and other nonprofits have different financial structures and use revenues differently; their quest for improvement and their treatment of employees and volunteers, however, must be exemplary—as an act of worship.

The Divine Dance

There is something special about outstanding choreography, in which skilled dancers blend motion and music and for a few moments transport their audience to another place. Beautiful dancing requires trust among partners and a certain disciplined risk, as all the dancers' movements intersect.

The triune life of God is a divine dance of mutual self-donation and shared delight. The Father is pleased for all fullness to dwell in the Son, and the Son honors the Father. The Holy Spirit is the uncreated bond of love between the Father and the Son and brings to each Christian and every gathered community the very presence of the Almighty.

When work goes well, it is like a well-prepared dance—with all participants fulfilling their part and bringing glory to God and good to others.

For the Boss: An Ethic of Service

The biblical instructions to the wealthy and powerful are clear and encouraging (Eph. 6:9; Col. 4:1; James 5:1–6). Employers will be judged for their ethics toward those under their supervision. The highest executive is still a servant of Christ, regardless of her or his company title (John 13). The Bible does not condemn levels of authority, or even wealth. What is clear is that Christian leaders must keep their commitments and create a positive environment for flourishing.

Economic exigencies determine prices and wages; nevertheless, there are many resources, both intangible and tangible, that a Christian leader can provide her or his employees. A joyful, caring, honest, and creative environment, accompanied by a philosophy of empowerment and opportunity, will result in potential workers lining up at the door. Profits matter, but service to customers and employees matter even more.

Leaders establish the purpose, vision, mission, values, goals, and structures of the company or enterprise. Though followers of Christ must never coerce religious affiliation, a company can be infused with Christian principles that inform all facets of the enterprise. The same entrepreneurial stewardship that informs company ethics and goals can overflow through business to transform communities and cities, and the ethos of empowerment transforms people and structures.

For the Employee: Work as Worship

Employees owe their bosses a full day's work, accompanied by a positive attitude and complete integrity. All Christians are "God's contractors" to their employer, whether they are permanent or temporary employees. In the paradoxical words of Martin Luther, "A Christian is master of all and slave to none. A Christian is master of none and slave to all." To work honestly and well, without bitterness or rancor, is noble service for the kingdom of God.

But what about work that is repetitive, toilsome, and barely provides for one's needs? This represents most work around the world and across time periods. The answer is not to glamorize laborious efforts, but to see God's purposes in the opportunities, relationships, and material provision work offers. There is always opportunity to pray for others, assist the struggling, and share the faith through actions and attitudes that honor God and distinguish Christian service.

Insight Three: New Measures of Success

Progress in Christian discipleship is measurable. Good calibration of biblical outcomes will lead to continual celebration of progress in our communities. We use a variety of measures to assess forward movement in our churches, denominations, and movements:

- ✧ Are our members growing in the spiritual disciplines, especially prayer, Bible reading, giving, and service?

- ✧ Are we seeing people come to Christ? Do our congregants know how to lead someone to Christ and offer basic discipleship foundations?

- ✧ Are we seeing believers baptized in water and baptized in the Holy Spirit?

- ✧ Are we seeing our congregants advance from being consumers of church services to contributors to our church's service to the world?

- ✧ Are we bringing hope to our congregation and community, and do our non-Christian neighbors respect our efforts?

- ✧ Do our members offer all parts of their daily lives to God as acts of worship, including marriage and family, work and play, and engagement in the broader society?

The burden of this entire work is that there is more—and we need to see economics and work in light of faith and develop their fruits. Here are some new "metrics" to complete our assessment of progress. The wonderful thing is that these flow out of a full understanding of the diagnostic questions listed above. Let's consider "counting" the following:

✧ Creative and innovative contributions at work

✧ Involvement in other community organizations

✧ New businesses started or current ones expanded

✧ Cultural impact, including participation in city-wide and regional events that enlighten and inspire creativity

✧ Involvement on local and regional leadership teams, such as school boards, city and county councils, and other public agencies

✧ Student success at all levels

✧ Involvement in the sports community, from helping young kids get started to coaching an advanced team

✧ Academic and intellectual leadership: new administrative or faculty appointments, writing, lecturing, etc.

✧ Political service as elected or appointed officials

The list is as numerous as the abilities, anointing, and opportunities God bestows.

The last bullet point makes some folks nervous. *Political* is a highly charged word. From a kingdom-of-God perspective, however, politics can be our godly involvement in helping our community to flourish. "Political" ultimately means public service (at least that is the aim). Local churches are permitted to help their members vote intelligently, with one legal caveat: specific candidates and parties may not be endorsed from official organs of the church. Candidates may be invited to speak, as long as all are invited. Vital issues can be addressed, and moral and social discernment is the obligation of leaders called to proclaim "the whole counsel of God." What is not permitted, either in Scripture or in legal statute, is partisanship that divides and often attacks the person as well as the principles under debate. It is a good thing for some in our congregations to enter the political world—accompanied by lots of prayer, accountability, and humility.

Back to Vocation and Occupation

All Christians have three divine vocations. We are worshipers of the triune God in all we do. We are witnesses, in word and deed, of the grace of Jesus Christ. And we are fashioned by our Creator and Redeemer for good works, ordained for each of us and each community. All believers have specific gifts, opportunities, and relationships they are able to invest for the glory of God and the good of others and for which they will give an account before the judgment seat of Christ (1 Cor. 3:10–15; 2 Cor. 5:10). These resources are the substance of one's calling or vocation.

We also have occupations—jobs—where we spend much of our waking hours. Whether in the home or office, factory or field, classroom or computer station, we work. Sometimes our sense of vocation and our current occupations are well-integrated and almost identical. Other times, we endure aspects of our daily work in service of our larger calling. In all cases, God honors all the efforts we bring to each day.

Discipleship that unites the Great Commandment and the Great Commission is lived out in and through our work. The local church is a community of Christ-followers in a particular place called to worship and witness in a particular way. Instead of separating "church" life from "regular" or "secular" life, we are the church in all domains of life—including work and participation in the economy.

The economy is nothing to be afraid of; it is the social framework in which our work finds value and we are able to flourish. Our stewardship of God's resources, from personal abilities to relational networks, is God's way of blessing the world and opening doors of opportunity to share the good news of Jesus Christ.

Holy Imagination

Transformation of church and society begin with the transformation of our thinking. The Bible tells us that our growth in holiness and in our vocation come when we allow the Lord to completely change our thinking, aligning every affection and thought according to the Word of God (Rom. 12:1–2; Eph. 4:22–24). The word for transformation in Greek is *metamorphosis*. This is not "new and improved" human insight, but complete, inside-out change arising from the new nature we have in Christ. We are now liberated for vision and service beyond our limited experiences and imaginations.

The Bible warns us not to chase fantasies or engage in ungodly speculation (Prov. 14:12–15; Col. 2:8; 1 Tim. 1:3–6). But we are encouraged to believe that our Lord can do more than we can ask or imagine when we place full trust in his grace and power and rely on his life (Eph. 3:20–21).

With prayer as our foundation, the wisdom of sisters and brothers as our frame, the history of the church as our electrical and water supply, let's imagine what kind of building we can construct if we unite these powerful resources with holy imaginations:

⬦ We begin a career-development ministry in our church or in tandem with other churches. In addition to assisting women and men of all ages acquire gainful employment, the aim would be to help them find focus in their vocations and fidelity in their relationships.

✧ Prayer at our altars includes wisdom for new initiatives at the office and for new open doors through community agencies.

✧ Commissioning for service now includes all occupations.

✧ We invite business, educational, social service, and religious leaders to roll-up-the-sleeves meetings that strategize on the welfare of our communities.

✧ As we plant new churches, we consider the economy of the next generation and seek God concerning our part in building a thriving community.

✧ Our foreign missionaries and global business leaders become friends and partners.

✧ We advocate for humane work conditions.

✧ We build strong marriages, because they are the leading indicator of future success for the children.

✧ Pastors are attentive to crises, but they find time to visit factory and field, office and classroom; and these visits increase understanding and transform preaching.

✧ Imagine all local churches, large and small, rural and urban, contemporary and traditional in style, integrating faith, work, and economics so that every congregation is salt and light for the Lord and even the enemies of the gospel speak well of the people of God.

Ready to Lead the Exploration?

Jesus Christ is the Creator and Sustainer who holds the universe together with his powerful, active word (Col. 1:15–20). He is also the Reconciler and Redeemer, inviting all of humankind to salvation (1 Cor. 1:20–31; 2 Cor. 5:14–21; 1 Tim. 2:1-6; 2 Peter 3:9). Our sovereign Lord became a servant in order that his transformed servants might share in his sovereignty, now and forever (Mark 10:35–45; John 1; 13; Rom. 8). In this age our reign with Christ is partial (2 Cor. 4:16–18), but it is real. In the age to come we will continue the experience of "glory to glory" (2 Cor. 3:18 KJV) as we explore and experience the array of God's beauty and works (Rev. 21–22).

For Spirit-filled Christians, this future glory visits us as we worship together, evangelize the lost, and see the supernatural demonstration of God's delivering and healing power confirm the gospel. The extraordinary plan and purpose of God through the church takes place through ordinary people who go to work and participate in the local and global economy every day. As leaders, our task is to awaken, commission, and empower God's people—rejoicing that this work touches all facets of life and creates flourishing churches and communities.

Study Questions

1. What new ideas for your neighborhood or community have been "percolating in prayer" as you seek to extend God's kingdom?
2. What pioneers do you admire? These can be women or men of faith, science, exploration, etc. What qualities stand out, and how are these instructive for us?
3. What life issues keep many in your congregation from flourishing? What resources need to be added to meet the needs?
4. What is the Spirit-led "next step" you will take as a result of reading and reflecting on this book?

For Further Reading

Clay, Doug. *Dreaming in 3D: Finding and Following God's Amazing Plan for Your Life*. Springfield, MO: Influence Resources, 2011.

Forster, Greg. *The Contested Public Square: The Crisis of Christianity and Politics.* Downers Grove, IL: InterVarsity, 2008.

Garrison, Alton. *The 360-Degree Disciple: Discipleship Going Full Circle.* Springfield, MO: Gospel Publishing House, 2012.

Veith, Gene Edward. *God at Work: Your Christian Vocation in All of Life.* Wheaton: Crossway, 2011.

Afterword

Our Story

We have an inescapable past but an incomparable future. God is not returning us to Eden but moving us toward the New Jerusalem. We are not souls trapped in bodies but human beings living the future now, in the power of the Spirit, in mortal bodies that will one day be eternal. We are not gods, but we are made in the image of the triune God and we are being remade in the likeness of Jesus Christ. Our eternal future is free from pain and tears, but it is more than an everlasting day off. We were made to work and create an economy so all can flourish. With the help of the Holy Spirit, we can be anointed administrators and artists, empowered educators and executives, Spirit-led homemakers and health care providers.

Our story can begin a new chapter today if we will read the Bible seriously, listen to our spiritual leaders attentively, pray earnestly, and trust wholeheartedly that the Lord has good plans for our lives here and now as well as a forever beyond our dreams. Everything we do can be offered as an act of worship: from private prayers to public speeches, from marital joy to ministry to the poor. We are all pebbles in the pond, sending ripples to the edges far beyond what we see. Our daily work can lead people closer to Christ, unleash productivity, and stimulate the economy—all tasks that God says are good.

The first-century church was not a superhero community, with "supermen" and "wonder women" roaming the world, zapping the bad guys, and performing amazing feats. No, the early church was a Spirit-empowered family of faith who knew the presence of God, understood the purpose of God, and aimed to walk in the holiness and power of God. They changed the world one relationship, one conversation, one act of mercy, and one deed of hard work at a time.

Remember, most of the original readers of the apostles' writings had no choice about their economic and social status, their location, or even their spouse. Yet God turned the world upside down through them. Yes, there were exorcisms, healings, and other miracles, which we should continue to expect in our lives today. But most of God's work took place as masters saw slaves rejoicing in God's grace, soldiers heard prisoners singing, and merchants found out they had an honest partner.

Let's begin the next chapter of our new story that weaves together faith, work, and economics—bringing glory to God, good to others, and gratitude to our souls.

Bibliography

Attanasi, Katherine, and Amos Yong, eds. *Pentecostalism and Prosperity.* New York: Palgrave-Macmillan, 2012.

Batterson, Mark. *The Circle Maker: Praying Circles Around Your Biggest Dreams and Greatest Fears.* Grand Rapids: Zondervan, 2011.

Blackard, Gary. *Relevance in the Workplace: Using the Bible to Impact Your Job.* Phoenix: Intermedia Publishing Group, 2011.

Buehring, Dave. *The Jesus Blueprint: Rediscovering His Original Plan for Changing the World.* Oviedo, FL: HigherLife Publishing, 2012.

Claar, Victor V., and Robin J. Klay. *Economics in Christian Perspective: Theory, Policy, and Life Choices.* Downers Grove, IL: InterVarsity, 2007.

Clarensau, Michael. *From Belonging to Becoming: The Power of Loving People Like Jesus Did.* Springfield, MO: Influence Resources, 2011.

Clay, Doug. *Dreaming in 3D: Finding and Following God's Amazing Plan for Your Life.* Springfield, MO: Influence Resources, 2011.

Corbett, Steve, and Brian Fikkert. *When Helping Hurts: How to Alleviate Poverty without Hurting the Poor . . . and Yourself.* 2nd ed. Chicago: Moody, 2012.

Forster, Greg. *The Contested Public Square: The Crisis of Christianity and Politics.* Downers Grove, IL: InterVarsity, 2008.

———. "Theology That Works," 2012. Available at the Oikonomia Network website, www.oikonomianetwork.org.

Foster, Richard J. *The Challenge of the Disciplined Life: Christian Reflections on Money, Sex, and Power.* New York: HarperCollins, 1985.

Fujimura, Makoto. *Refractions: A Journey of Faith, Art and Culture.* Colorado Springs: NavPress, 2009.

Garrison, Alton. *The 360-Degree Disciple: Discipleship Going Full Circle.* Springfield, MO: Gospel Publishing House, 2012.

Hart, David Bentley. *Atheist Delusions: The Christian Revolution and Its Fashionable Enemies.* New Haven: Yale University Press, 2010.

Hewitt, Les, and Charlie Self. *The Power of Faithful Focus.* Deerfield, FL: Faith Communications, 2004.

Hill, Jonathan. *What Has Christianity Ever Done for Us? How It Shaped the Modern World.* Downers Grove, IL: InterVarsity, 2005.

Jarrett, Bryan. *Extravagant: Living Out Your Response to God's Outrageous Love.* Springfield, MO: Influence Resources, 2011.

Johnson, Brett. *Ministry of Business Bible Study.* Saratoga, CA: The Institute for Innovation, Integration & Impact, 2011.

———. *Repurposing Capital.* Saratoga, CA: Indaba Publishing, 2010.

Johnson, Brett, and Lyn Johnson. *Convergence.* Saratoga, CA: Indaba Publishing, 2010.

Keller, Tim. *Center Church: Doing Balanced, Gospel-Centered Ministry in Your City.* Grand Rapids: Zondervan, 2012.

Levy, David. *Gray Matter: A Neurosurgeon Discovers the Power of Prayer . . . One Patient at a Time.* Carol Stream, IL: Tyndale, 2011.

McGinnis, Alan Loy. *The Friendship Factor: How to Get Closer to the People You Care For.* Philadelphia: Augsburg Fortress, 2004.

Miller, Donald E., and Tetsunao Yamamori. *Global Pentecostalism: The New Face of Social Engagement.* Berkeley: University of California Press, 2007.

Noll, Mark. *Jesus Christ and the Life of the Mind.* Grand Rapids: Eerdmans, 2011.

Peterson, Eugene. *Practice Resurrection: A Conversation on Growing Up in Christ.* Grand Rapids: Eerdmans, 2010.

Ridderbos, Herman N. *The Coming of the Kingdom.* Edited by Raymond O. Zorn. Translated by H. de Jongste. Phillipsburg, NJ: Presbyterian & Reformed, 1962.

Robeck, Cecil M., Jr. *The Azusa Street Mission and Revival: The Birth of the Global Pentecostal Movement.* Nashville: Thomas Nelson, 2006.

Robison, James, and Jay W. Richards. *Indivisible: Restoring Faith, Family, and Liberty Before It Is Too Late.* New York: FaithWords, 2012.

Roxburgh, Alan J., and Fred Romanuk. *The Missional Leader: Equipping Your Church to Reach a Changing World.* New York: Jossey-Bass, 2006.

Samuel, Vinay, and Chris Sugden, eds. *Mission as Transformation: A Theology of the Whole Gospel.* Oxford: Regnum, 2009.

Scazzero, Peter. *The Emotionally Healthy Church: A Strategy for Discipleship That Actually Changes Lives.* Grand Rapids: Zondervan, 2010.

Sheiman, Bruce. *An Atheist Defends Religion: Why Humanity Is Better Off with Religion Than without It.* New York: Alpha, 2009.

Sowell, Thomas. *Economic Facts and Fallacies.* New York: Basic Books, 2008.

Stark, Rodney. *For the Glory of God: How Monotheism Led to Reformations, Science, Witch-Hunts, and the End of Slavery.* Princeton, NJ: Princeton University Press, 2004.

Stearns, Richard. *The Hole in the Gospel.* Nashville: Thomas Nelson, 2010.

Tozer, A. W. *The Knowledge of the Holy: The Attributes of God: Their Meaning in the Christian Life.* New York: HarperCollins, 1978.

Valci, Roger. "God's Empowering Presence," "Our Rule of Life," and "The Meeting"—three tracts available at the Valley Christian Center website, www.comediscovervcc.org.

Veith, Gene Edward. *God at Work: Your Christian Vocation in All of Life.* Wheaton: Crossway, 2011.

Webber, Robert. *Who Gets to Narrate the World? Contending for the Christian Story in an Age of Rivals.* Downers Grove, IL: InterVarsity, 2008.

Willard, Dallas. *The Great Omission: Rediscovering Jesus' Essential Teachings on Discipleship.* San Francisco: HarperCollins, 2006.

Yong, Amos. *Who Is the Holy Spirit? A Walk with the Apostles.* Brewster, MA: Paraclete, 2011.

Zimmermann, Jens. *Incarnational Humanism: A Philosophy of Culture for the Church in the World.* Downers Grove, IL: InterVarsity, 2012.

About the Author

Charlie Self is professor of church history at Evangel University in Springfield, Missouri. Prior to his joining the faculty at Evangel, he served for thirty years in various pastoral roles—including senior pastor—and concurrently taught for twenty-eight years at Bethany University, Western Seminary, George Fox University, and Continental Theological Seminary in Brussels, Belgium.

Made in the USA
Middletown, DE
21 April 2019